Tuḥfat al-Mujāhidīn

SHAYKH ZAINUDDIN MAKHDUM

Tuḥfat al-Mujāhidīn

A Historical Epic of the Sixteenth Century

Translated from Arabic with annotations by
S Muhammad Husayn Nainar

Islamic Book Trust
Kuala Lumpur

ISBN 983-9154-80-X / 978-983-9154-80-1

Jointly published 2006 by
Islamic Book Trust, Kuala Lumpur and Other Books, Calicut.

Islamic Book Trust
607 Mutiara Majestic
Jalan Othman
46000 Petaling Jaya
Malaysia
www.ibtbooks.com
Tel: 603-77813197
Email: *ibtkl@streamyx.com*

Other Books
P.O.Box No. 620
New Way Building
Railway Link Road
Kozhikode
Kerala 673002, India
Tel: 91-495-2306808
Email: *otherbooks@post.com*

Publisher's Note

The importance of Shaykh Zainuddin's *Tuḥfat al-Mujāhidīn,* as a source book of European colonial history, cannot be overemphasised. Yet, to our knowledge, there is no English translation of this book now extant. This prompted us to undertake the task of bringing out an English translation of the book, as English is now recognised as one of the leading languages for Islamic studies.

For practical reasons, we decided to bring out an English version of the book from a Malayalam translation. Malayalam is the language of Malabar, where all the incidents of Portuguese encroachments into India, described in the book, took place. For this we chose a recently published Malayalam translation by C. Hamza. This is an extensively annotated translation containing more than 200 scholarly notes, explaining local backgrounds and identifying, clearly and convincingly, the places and people mentioned in the book.

Dr A.I. Vilayathullah, an English teacher, graciously undertook the translation and completed his assignment early in 2005. We were all set to bring out the book when, unexpectedly, we received a hardly readable photocopy of an earlier translation of the book with few pages missing. This was a translation by S. Muhammad Husayn Nainar, published in Madras in 1942. On comparing this translation, which was done directly from the Arabic original, with our new translation which was from

Malayalam, we realized the incongruity of translating a work from a secondary source, one step removed from the original work.

This made us to rethink our project and we decided to republish Nainar's translation, duly edited and upgraded. In revising Nainar's translation, we have consulted the Arabic original throughout, and corrected many mistranslations and inconsistencies found in it to make sure that this edition will be the most faithful translation of the Arabic original of *Tuḥfat al-Mujāhidīn*. As regards the notes, we took in all the notes in C. Hamza's Malayalam edition as already translated by Dr Vilayathullah and added them to the book as endnotes while retaining Nainar's footnotes without any change, except that some of his long notes had to be incorporated in the endnotes appropriately marked "Nainar" in brackets.

A word about typography. Names of persons and places, as well as Arabic words have been transliterated from the original using the current transliteration system. While this reflects the correct pronunciation of these words in Arabic, there is, however, exception to some words and names, such as for names of the Moghul sultans and of places in India. These are mentioned in many other books in their anglicized form and therefore using the diacritical system would mean difficulty for reference or research purposes. This may also defeat the purpose of this edition, which is to relate the various names of places and persons mentioned in the Arabic original to contemporary history.

This edition came to fruition through the combined effort of many people. The idea of an English version of *Tuḥfat* occurred to me after seeing the Malayalam version, translated by C. Hamza, which was presented to me together with the

Arabic original, by my friend Dr Ausaf Ahsan of Manipal, India. Dr Ausaf also secured for us the help of Dr Vilayathullah to begin the work in the first place. Although we had largely abandoned Vilayathullah's version of the *Tuhfat* text, his efforts had not been in vain. His translation had been of immense help in editing and improving Nainar's version. Half of this book is still his work as all the endnotes incorporated here are translated by him from the Malayalam edition. He also wrote a short biography of Zainuddin Makhdum, the author of the *Tuhfat*.

We are also indebted to Mr N.M. Husain who provided us the photocopy of Nainar's edition in the nick of time. Finally our heartfelt gratitude to Dr K.K.N. Kurup for writing a Foreword for this edition as he had written for the Malayalam translation.

P.K. Koya Kutty,
Islamic Book Trust,
Kuala Lumpur
June 2006.

Contents

List of Photographs and Illustrations

- Vasco da Gama; Alfonso de Albuquerque.
- Kappad beach where Portuguese navigator Vasco da Gama arrived in 1498; a monument marks the spot where he landed.
- An illustration of a ship of the sixteenth century, similar to those used by the Portuguese explorers; the *Savo Gabriel*, the ship used by the Portuguese.
- Front view of the Kunjali Marakkar mosque, Iringal, Kottakkal, Calicut.
- Top structure of the Kunjali Marakkar mosque; a view from the interior of the top structure, where Kunjali Marakkar used as a watching tower to detect the movement of the Portuguese fleet.
- An illustration of the Portuguese fort at Calicut; Kotta, the town and fort of the Kunjalis.
- The *mimbar* in the Kunjali Marakkar Masjid is the throne captured by Kunjali Marakkar from a Portuguese ship; close-up of carved decorations on the *mimbar*, showing, among others, images of eagles and a queen.
- A panorama of Calicut shows several types of ships, shipbuilding, net fishing, dinghy traffic and a rugged, sparsely populated interior.

- Ancient calendar on the walls of the Kunjali Marakkar mosque, written in Arabi-Malayalam and ancient Malayalam scripts.
- An interior view of the Kunjali Marakkar mosque; the traditional Indian lamp inside the Kunjali Marakkar mosque.
- A section of Kunjali Marakkar High School in Iringal, Kottakkal, Calicut.
- Kunjali Marakkar's residence, rebuilt by the Indian government.
- Kunjali Marakkar's sword, said to be captured from the Portuguese; a shield used by Kunjali Marakkar in the battles against the Portuguese.
- The Kunhipalli mosque near Mahi, where Shaykh Zainuddin Makhdum is said to be buried.
- The spot where the author, Shaykh Zainuddin, is believed to be buried, at the Kunhipalli mosque.

Foreword

The Arab tradition in historical writings has been well acclaimed for its characteristic features of minute observation, narration and analysis. Since the days of Ibn Khaldūn, geography, history, ethics and theology had influenced the mindsets of the scholars in the Arab world and opened new vistas of culture and humanism. Such trends were gradually spread to different countries and regions where the socio-cultural milieu of the Arabs were transplanted.

This Arab tradition in the sixteenth century had made significant contributions to the knowledge system through reputed scholars and creative writers in theology, poetry, art and religion from different regions. Kerala is one such region where the Makhdum family made its landmark by projecting a theoretical and pragmatic approach to counter the European adventurers against Islam and its followers. Shaykh Zainuddin Makhdum the Junior, and the first Keralite historian gives an ideological interpretation to the long struggle against Portuguese expansion and its programme of effecting colonial settlements. His major historical work, *Tuḥfat al-Mujāhidīn* (Glory to the Victory of Martyrs) written mainly after 1583 AD deals with the chronological, political and military accounts of the Zamorins of Calicut and their naval commandants, the Kunjalis, in their fight against the Portuguese.

The introduction by the author sets forth the reasons which compelled him to write this historical work. It is mainly to stir the Muslims into a *jihād* against the Portuguese who oppressed the Muslims and natives of Malabar. In the first chapter, he traces the merits of *jihād* giving verses of the Qur'an. The second chapter gives an account of the emergence of the Muslim community in Malabar. In the third, the author narrates the customs and manners of the indigenous people. After these three chapters, he gives a detailed account of the Portuguese advent in 1498 AD till 1583 AD. Such details lead us to the life and conditions of the Muslims in Kerala. Before the arrival of the Portuguese, the Muslims enjoyed respect and prosperity in this region. The Portuguese arrival spelled the end of their trade superiority and monopoly in coastal trade. As a community, they also lost their vigour for martial activities including *jihād*. Subsequently the Portuguese influence became dominant.

As such the work has a central theme to initiate a *jihād* against the oppressors and enemies so that the community can live in peace and prosperity. Here the concept of *jihād* is projected not to dethrone the Zamorin or to capture his territories, but to seek a peaceful life for the Islamic community in a *dār al-ḥarb* (non-Islamic country).

This historical work has been earlier translated into English by Lieut. M.J. Rawlandson in 1833. The fourth chapter of the work dealing with the Portuguese affairs had been translated into Portuguese by David Lopez. Scholars such as Emerson and James Briggs translated this work into English.

An Arabic text of this work was edited by Hakim Shamsullah Qadiri in 1931 from Hyderabad. He also translated some portions into Urdu. The work in Arabic, which was already published from Lisbon, also appeared in Latin, French, Spanish and Czech. It also came out in the Indian languages like Malayalam, Kanares and Tamil. In Malayalam, it was done by Velayudhan Panikkasseri (with a modified title) in 1963 and

C. Hamza in 1995. As early as in 1936, K. Moossankutty Moulavi brought out an Arabi-Malayalam text of this work.

Mohammed Quasim Ferishta in his Persian work, *Tareekh-e-Ferishta* (Lucknow, 1864) incorporated extracts from this work of Zainuddin, although it takes us back to the year 1611 AD. These inclusions after 1583 might be the work of some one else. (See James Briggs, trans. *History of the Rise of the Mohammedan Power in India till 1612*, IV).

This Arabic text, written in the last quarter of the sixteenth century, is used to teach the students in Dars and other institutions of Islamic community. As such several local variations of the text were also available due to the spread in the form of calligraph or manuscript. In 1942 an authentic translation into English by S. Muhammad Husayn Nainar was published by the University of Madras based on the text edited by Shamsullah Qadiri. The translator had also given extensive notes, but did not alter or add the names of places in the body of the text. For instance they remained as Kalikut, Kashi (Cochin) Purtukal (Portugal) Fakkanur (Barkur), Darmfatan (Darmadam) Banjala (Bengal) etc, as originally used by the author.

In the present edition, the liberty taken to replace those names with the modern names has rendered the book more readable. The new elaborate and descriptive endnotes on men, events, places, Islamic theology and Qur'anic verses also help the readers for a proper understanding of the narrative accounts by Zainuddin; the efforts taken in this direction has made this edition to be praiseworthy.

It is believed that Zainuddin tried his best to create a confederacy of Muslim rulers against the Portuguese incorporating the Sultans of Egypt, Gujarat and Bijapur alongside the Zamorin of Calicut as kingpin of the allies. His diplomatic role as a historian and as a defender of Islam was evidently the strength and inspiration for the prolonged maritime encounters of the Kunjali Marakkars, the veteran commodores of Calicut. He always appreciated the enthusiasm of the Zamorin and his devotion to the cause of the Muslims. He could also see the lack of enthusiasm among the Muslim rulers of the Deccan fighting against the Portuguese, the inveterate foes of the Muslims.

Zainuddin selected Ali Adil Shah (1558-1580) of Bijapur as his patron. That is why the work was dedicated with a glorious tribute to his patron whom he considered "a zealous monarch, hearty and persistent in his endeavour to propagate the Faith and root out the enemies of Islam".

The legacy of Islam finally elevated Zainuddin to the galaxy of great Sufis of Malabar for his devotion to the propagation of Islam and his commitment to the cause of fellow religious men of Kerala. His tomb at Chombal, in the mosque of Kunhippalli, is revered by all communities irrespective of their religion.

The republication of this anti-colonial manifesto appears at a time when global conflicts are taking place among different religious groups and fundamentalists. The breeding ground of these conflicts are not religious aspirations, but efforts to accumulate wealth and resources as in the sixteenth century by superior nations. The spirit of Islam resisted those encroachments on human dignity and culture. Such a valuable lesson could never be gone into oblivion and it demands devotion and dedication by generations after generations.

Dr K.K.N. Kurup
(Former Vice Chancellor University of Calicut)
Director, Malabar Institute for Research & Development,
Vatakara,
July 2005.

Short Biography of Shaykh Zainuddin

Tuḥfat al-Mujāhidīn is a pioneering historical work written in the ninth century AH (sixteenth century AD). It is the first authentic work on the history of Kerala and has survived in its original shape. It has been naturally subjected to meticulous and judicious evaluations by academic historians.

Shaykh Zainuddin Makhdum, the author of *Tuḥfat al-Mujāhidīn*, also known as Shaykh Zainuddin Makhdum II, was born at Chombal, near Mahe, Northern Malabar, India, in the ninth century AH. He was the grandson of Shaykh Zainuddin Makhdum I, a well known scholar of Ḥadīth, author, poet, and a vehement champion of the anti-imperialist struggles.

The roots of the Makhdum family were in Ma'bar, in Yemen. From there, they arrived at places like Keelakkara, Kayal Pattanam, etc., in Tamil Nadu. This family had a big role in the spread of Islam in places like Madurai, Tanjaur, Tiruchirapally, Nagur, etc.

The Makhdum family arrived at Ponnani and settled down there in the early ninth century AH. The first of the Makhdums to arrive at Ponnani was Shaykh Zayn al-Dīn Ibrāhīm bin Aḥmad. He was a paternal uncle of Shaykh Zainuddin Makhdum I. Ponnani had ties with the Arabs through trade since ancient times. It came to be known as the Makkah of Kerala Muslims ever since the Makhdums began their religious and educational activities there. Before long, Ponnani occupied the religious leadership of the Muslims of Kerala. It was Shaykh Zainuddin I who built the famous big *jum'ah* mosque of Ponnani and began there the reputed centre of religious learning.

Shaykh Zainuddin Makhdum II was the first son of the famous scholar Shaykh Muhammad al-Ghazali, the third son of Zainuddin I. Shaykh Muhammad al-Ghazali was the *muftī* (scholar who gives religious verdicts and opinions) and *qāḍī qudāh* (judge of judges or chief of religious judges) of Northern Malabar. It was he who built the big *jum'ah* mosque in Chombal near Mahe. He was the first *qāḍī* as well as *khaṭīb* (one who gives Friday sermons) of this mosque. His wife, Zainuddin's mother, was an extremely pious and virtuous lady of the Waliyakat Taraketti Tarawad of Chombal. There are those who believe that Zainuddin was born in Ponnani, his father's place. However, no documental evidence is available for establishing either of these opinions.

Zainuddin was brought up in the religious environment of the family. He had his primary education at home at the hands of his scholarly parents. After his primary education at home, Zainuddin was enrolled at the Ponnani *jum'ah* mosque's *daras* (class) for further education. He was taught there mainly by Shaykh Abdul Aziz Makhdum, his paternal uncle and a well-known scholar. Besides other subjects, Zainuddin memorised here the whole Qur'an to become a *ḥāfiz*.

After completing his education at Ponnani, Zainuddin set out to Makkah in a cargo ship to perform the hajj and seek further education. After performing the hajj and visiting Madīnah, he spent nearly ten years in Makkah pursuing higher learning. He was able to master all branches of Islamic learning directly from the well known scholars of Makkah. His deep knowledge in *ahādīth* earned him the title of *muhaddith*. One of his important teachers at Makkah was Imām Shihāb al-Dīn Aḥmad bin Ḥājar al-Haytamī al-Makkī, a renowned author and scholar of the Shāfi'ī school of Islamic jurisprudence. Shaykh al-Islām 'Izz al-Dīn bin 'Abd al-'Azīz al-Zumarī, 'Allāmah Wajīh al-Dīn 'Abd al-Raḥmān bin Ziyād, and Shaykh al-Islām 'Abd al-Raḥmān bin Ṣafā were among his other important teachers there.

Shaykh Zainuddin learned *taṣawwuf* from Abū al-Ḥasan al-Ṣiddīq al-Bakarī. It is said that Shaykh al-Bakarī honoured him in special way and made him an accepted *shaykh* of the Qādiriyyah sufi order.

Back from Makkah, Shaykh Zainuddin began to strive for the cause of education and reformation within the Muslim community and started teaching at the *madrasah* for higher education at the Ponnani mosque, serving as its *mudarris* (teacher) even during the lifetime of Shaykh Abdul Aziz Makhdum, second son of his paternal uncle Zainuddin Makhdum I. He taught there for 36 years. Besides being a great scholar and inspiring teacher, Zainuddin was also a powerful orator.

Another important aspect of Zainuddin's personality is revealed from his continuing rapport with the great scholars of the Islamic world of the time. The most eminent among them was 'Allāmah Ibn Ḥājar al-Haytamī, his teacher at Makkah. It is said that al-Haytamī honoured Zainuddin by making a trip to Ponnani all the way from Makkah and staying with him for a period. Manuscripts of al-Haytamī's *fatwās* issued during the visit are still preserved carefully. Other great scholars with whom he maintained contact through regular correspondence were some of his friends and fellow students at Makkah. Imām Muḥammad Ramlī and Imām Muḥammad Khaṭīb al-Sarwīnī were among them. Zainuddin was used to writing letters to them in verses in Arabic. His circle of friends included state leaders and men of consequences from all over the world. He had close personal relationship with the Mughal King Akbar, Bijapur Sultan Ibrahim Ali Adil Shah, Muhammad Ali Adil Shah, the Zamorin of Calicut, etc. He had often been the Zamorin's envoy to the rulers of the Islamic countries, like Egypt and Turkey, with the king's requests for military help against the Portuguese. The Zamorin often depended on Zainuddin to correspond in Arabic with the Arab rulers of the time.

Shaykh Zainuddin II's contribution to Islamic learning, like that of his grandfather Zainuddin I, was immense. He wrote several erudite works on many topics related to Islam. His work on Islamic jurisprudence *Fatḥ al-Muʿīn fī Sharahi Qurratil-ʿAyn* is well-known. Published from several parts of the Islamic world in many editions, the book is an enlarged and revised version of his earlier work *Qurratul ʿAyn* which had fascinated several Islamic scholars of the time. Many learned men of subsequent generations had written lengthy volumes interpretting it. It is even today used as a textbook in many Islamic institutes in India.

Another eminent work by Zainuddin II is *Irshād al-ʿIbādah*, a book on *taṣawwuf,* published several times from Egypt. *Al-Ajwibatul ʿAjībah, Aḥkām al-Nikāḥ* and *al-Manhaj al-Wāḍiḥ,* published in various editions from Malabar, are among his other renowned works.

There is no authentic information as to the date of Zainuddin's death. The famous Egyptian scholar and historian Shaykh Muḥammad ʿAbd al-Munʿin al-Numayrī documents in his *Tārīkh al-Islam fī al-Hind* that Zainuddin died in 991 AH. George Zaidan's work on literary history *Tārīkh al-Adabī Lughatil ʿArabiyyah,* however, places his death in 978 AH. That Shaykh Zainuddin and his wife were buried in the graveyard attached to the little mosque of Chombal and that they had three children (Abu Bakar, Abdul Aziz and Fatimah) are clear from the documents with the local historians.

Tuḥfat al-Mujāhidīn, the historical work in Arabic language, is his best known work. It is noted for its unique significance among the studies and works on Portuguese colonialism. It talks mainly about the Portuguese attempts to colonise the coastal territories of Kerala and a century long resistance to it led mainly by the Muslim community in the region.

It is the first book ever written on the history of Kerala. It is based on the author's own first hand information of events and things and what he could gather from reliable sources. As the author makes clear in the Preface, it was written with the object of motivating the Muslims for the struggle against the invading Portuguese. It also explains at length the philosophical grounds of *jihād*, and, quoting Qur'an and Ḥadīth, the necessity for the Muslim community to be prepared for it. Here, in Zainuddin, one can see a brave, patriotic and level-headed scholar who rises to the occasion giving his people the right kind of leadership that is expected of a great scholar with a historical mission.

The book also talks about the early history of the advent and spread of Islam in Malabar. It is the earliest historical document that could be relied on for learning about the customs and practices of the Hindu society of Malabar. The most important section of the book is the fourth, consisting of fourteen chapters, that truthfully describes the Malabar people's heroic resistance to the Portuguese invasion under the Zamorins and the Kunhalis. They are among the glorious episodes of the history of the global Muslim community. Its influence on the historic beginning of the Indian struggle for independence can be seen from the fact that the struggles against the British colonizers in the region sought inspiration by singing eulogies in admiration of the brave resistance of the Kunhalis to the Portuguese invasion.

As a historical document, *Tuḥfat al-Mujāhidīn* is of inestimable value. It was first published in its Arabic original from Lisbon. A copy of it is preserved in the library of Al-Azhar University, Cairo, Egypt. Several sections of the book appeared in translations on various occasions, in Portuguese, Latin, French, German, Spanish, Persian, English etc. It has been translated into Malayalam, Urdu, Gujarati, Kannada, Tamil and other Indian languages. It used to be a textbook for study in the Islamic institutes of Malabar for several years.

Its importance as a unique historical document dealing with the rise of Malabar as a medieval naval force under the Kunhalis and the Malabar-Portuguese struggles between 1498 and 1583 has been unanimously acclaimed by scholars and historians. The book has been uniquely noted for the absolute honesty and objectivity that the author maintained in reporting the events.

For the global Muslim community, the book is of unique importance in another way. It talks about a long drawn out heroic and successful struggle against Portuguese imperialism at a time their future looked very bleak and they had been facing setbacks and failures all over the world. The success of the Malabar Muslims, a negligible force in comparison, in their struggles against the Portuguese, the foremost imperialistic power of the time, will be inspiring to the present generation, *inshā' Allāh*. Further, it establishes, once and for all, the fact that Islam and the Muslim community have always been considered an obstacle to the imperialistic ambitions of all times, the Portuguese and the British in the past or the U.S. and its allies in the modern times. The book is an invaluable achievement in Islamic historiography and a rich addition to its glorious tradition. *Tuḥfat al-Mujāhidīn*, thus, is compulsory reading for anybody trying to learn about the post-Cordova episodes of the history of the global Islamic movement.

Dr A.I. Vilayathullah

Translator's Preface

$\mathfrak{I}$t seems almost unnecessary to state that the *Tuḥfat al-Mujāhidīn* has already been translated into English by Lieut. M.J. Rowlandson as early as 1833 A.D.[a] But few books have fallen into oblivion as this one. Not only Arabists have almost forgotten this work, but the geographical information provided by it has not been fully utilised in any scheme of study of the ancient seaports of Southern India, though, not infrequently, some passing reference to this work is made by scholars.

The translation now offered to the public was begun many years ago, but its progress was so retarded by difficulties of text and other causes that it could not be got out in a form ready for publication. During the visit of the present translator to England about three years ago, he had the opportunity to consult two other texts of the same work in the India Office Library, London, and collate his copy with them. Yet the text was not at all satisfactory in regard to the quotations from the Qur'an and Ḥadīth (Traditions) of the Prophet. Even a recent edition[b] of this

---

a. Lieut. M. J. Rowlandson, Cor. M.R.A.S., Persian Interpreter to the Head-quarters of the army, Fort St. George, translated the work into English. It was printed by J. L. Cox & Son, 75, Great Queen Street, London, for the Oriental Translation Fund of Great Britain and Ireland, and sold by John Murray, Albemarle Street, and Parbury, Allen & Co, Leaden-hall Street, London, 1833 AD.

b. The Arabic text was edited by Ḥakīm Shamsullāh Qādirī, Hyderabad, Deccan, 1931 work was published without the First Chapter which abounds in quotations from the Qur'an and Ḥadīth.

The translator first set himself to the task of examining the accuracy of the text pertaining to the First Chapter, with good and reliable editions of books on Traditions and also checked the references to the verses of the Qur'an.

Alongside of the difficulty in regard to the text of Ḥadīth, the presence of a large number of place names, mostly of Dravidian origin, deterred the scholars from taking to the work wholeheartedly. These names are transliterated in Arabic in singularly crude and obscure forms in all the available copies in India and England, and their identification becomes very difficult. A familiar acquaintance with Dravidian languages and also with the geographical information supplied by the Arabic literature is absolutely necessary to arrive at proper conclusions in regard to the identification of these place names. Whatever the present translator has achieved in that direction, he owes it to the results of his study of the Arab geographers, and a large portion of his conclusions regarding place names would not have been possible without the information collected for the study mentioned above. In justification of these conclusions in the present book, the translator would refer the kind reader to his work *Arabs' Knowledge of Southern India*[a] and especially the first chapter on Geography. These conclusions would not only give information about a place, whose original name has undergone a curious change in the mouths of Arab navigators and merchants and remained all these years a puzzle to scholars, but would, it is believed, promote further study to secure accuracy about the identification. No doubt mistakes might have crept in, but as far as the information at the translator's disposal

---

a. The work was published in 1942 by the University of Madras.

and his ability to use it are concerned, his identification about place names may be taken as fairly correct.

Now a few words may be said about the work. Although the *Tuḥfat al-Mujāhidīn* is a brief narrative, it is remarkable for the information contained in it, and it constitutes an important addition to our knowledge of the geography of Southern India and the beginning of the Portuguese history in India. It gives us a clear picture of the earlier activities of the Portuguese in Malabar. As the account is now rendered into English, it is unnecessary to discuss or analyse the details here and it will be sufficient to note a few points.

The work consists of an Introduction and Four Sections.

The Introduction sets forth the reasons which led the author to compile this narrative, chiefly to stir up the Muslims into activity against the unbelievers who had invaded the territories of the Muslims and oppressed them.

The *First Section* deals with the merits of *jihād,* giving the verses of the Qur'an and the sayings of the Prophet that relate to the rewards for those who engage themselves in holy war against unbelievers.

The *Second Section* gives an account of the first appearance of Islam in Malabar, and the growth of various prosperous seaports on the West Coast.

In the *Third Section*, the author enumerates the strange usages and customs of the Hindu inhabitants of Malabar and the treatment accorded to the Muslim subjects by the Hindu rulers.

After these three sections, which comprise nearly half of the narrative, commences the *Fourth Section.* This portion is entirely historical giving an account of the Portuguese from the time of their first arrival in Malabar in 1498 AD right up to 1583 AD, covering a period of about eighty-five years. The details contained in this section lead one to emphasise four features in particular.

Firstly, the Muslims, before the advent of the Portuguese, appear to have been in good condition, and they were treated by the Hindu rulers with great respect and consideration; secondly, as a result of the Portuguese competition, the Muslims lost their trade supremacy and were no longer the sole carriers of trade to the west; thirdly, the martial vigour of the Muslims began to decline along with their fervent faith; fourthly, the Portuguese influence became all powerful in due course.

Thus with the rise of the Portuguese influence, the prosperity of the Muslims declined. The Portuguese opposed the Muslims, reduced them to misery and treated them with contempt in almost every respect. The narrative reveals a base description of their behaviour towards the Muslims. But the enthusiasm of the Zamorin of Calicut, and his devotion to the cause of the Muslims, were always unbounded. He spared neither men nor money in fighting against the Portuguese, the inveterate foes of the Muslims. Among the Muslim rulers in the Deccan, on the other hand, there was lack of enthusiasm or affinity for the interests of their Muslim brethren, a fact much deplored by the author of this work. No doubt some Muslim Sultans of the period did come forward to fight against the Portuguese, but they did not make much progress.

Of Shaykh Zainuddin, the author of the *Tuḥfat al-Mujāhidīn*, very little is known. His full name is Shaykh Zainuddin, son of Abdul Aziz, son of Zainuddin, son of Ali, son of Ahmad al-Ma'bari. The term al-Ma'bari indicates that his ancestors belonged to Ma'bar.

Ma'bar is an Arabic word used for the first time by Yāqūt (1179-1229) in his *Geographical Dictionary* to denote the east coast of the Indian peninsula. It is not possible from the accounts of Yāqūt and other Arab geographers to locate exactly where, at what point the east coast (Ma'bar) begins, and the exact area it comprises along that coast. Abū al-Fidā' says that Ma'bar begins at about three or four days' journey to the east of Kawlam (Quilon) and the first locality from the side of Malībār (Malabar) is Rās Kumhurī (Cape Comorin).[a]

Thus Ma'bar, the east coast of the Indian peninsula, seems to be the ancestral home of Shaykh Zainuddin. Ahmad, his ancestor, appears to have been the original immigrant to Ma'bar. Evidently he gave himself the appellation 'al-Ma'bari'[b] when he began to move from place to place. Shaykh Zainuddin who is said to have lived in Ponnani, Malabar district, also retained that title to suggest his ancestral home.

It appears from the work that Shaykh Zainuddin must have lived during the period of Ali Adil Shah (1558-1580) whom the *shaykh* selected as his patron. Ferishta, the celebrated historian of that period, who has a chapter on "The Mahomedans in Malabar" in his book,[c] says: "All the materials of the history of the Mahomedans of the Malabar coast that I have been able to collect, are derived from *Tohfut-ool-Mujahideen.*" But he does not mention the name of the author of that work. His silence is rather remarkable.

The whole chapter of Ferishta does not exceed twelve pages.[d] It gives a brief account of the introduction of Islam in Malabar, and the proceedings of the Portuguese there. A reading of this chapter inclines one to ask whether Ferishta could have summarised from Shaykh Zainuddin's work. It is generally

---

a. For detailed information on Ma'bar see my *Arabs' Knowledge of Southern India*, pp. 53-56.
b. The term means one who belongs to Ma'bar.
c. *History of the Rise of the Mohammedan Power in India till the year 1612.* Translated from the original Persian of Mahomed Kasim Ferishta by John Briggs, Vol. IV.
d. Briggs' English Translation, Vol. IV, pp. 531-541.

understood that even the most rigorous summary of a long account must retain the essentials of the original. But in this case there is disparity between the two. The most conspicuous difference is, while the *shaykh's* narrative stops with the year 1583 AD, Ferishta's takes us to 1611 AD. Besides, Ferishta's account contains references to the prevalence of Shāfi'ism in Malabar, speaks of the Nāiṭ community, and mentions the grant by the Emperor Jahangir (1605-1627) to the English of a plot in Surat for the purpose of their building a factory. All these facts lead one to the view that the *Tuḥfat al-Mujāhidīn,* from which Ferishta took extracts, might be the work of some one else, and not the book of Shaykh Zainuddin. The question has to be investigated further with great care.

The ancestors of Shaykh Zainuddin might have immigrated to Ma'bar from some part of the Islamic empire in the fifteenth century, for the *shaykh* who wrote his book in the sixteenth century, was a descendant in the fifth degree of Ahmad, who was the first to style himself as 'al-Ma'bari'.

Shaykh Zainuddin is said to have written many books and commentaries, but definite information on these is not yet available. But it can be inferred from the present work that the *shaykh* was genuinely pious, self-respecting and independent. His style is very simple and direct without rhetorical ornament, yet he is not free from the affectation of ornate style so common with most theologians who had steeped their minds in the Qur'an and Ḥadīth.

To these meagre particulars of Shaykh Zainuddin's life, it may be added that the *shaykh* believed in pan-Islamism, for he not only incites the Muslim Sultans of the Deccan to action against the *unbelievers (Portuguese) by politely-worded remonstrance, but he has, with a glorious tribute, dedicated his work to Ali Adil Shah, whom he considers as a zealous monarch, hearty and persistent in his endeavour to propagate the Faith, and root out the enemies of Islam.

A few words may probably be expected here on the English translation of the *Tuḥfat al-Mujāhidīn* by Lieut. M.J. Rowlandson, Persian interpreter to the Headquarters of the army, Madras. It is clear the Lieutenant did the English translation about a century ago under conditions that were different from what we know today. Yet he brought out an admirable publication. Perhaps the critic who is disposed to scrutinise it closely will feel the need for a fresh English rendering from the original Arabic in the form as it is now offered to the public; also he will not be reluctant to admit the fact that considerable progress has been made in the present publication in regard to the identification of numerous names of persons and places that occur in the book.

Before concluding it must be mentioned that the *Tuḥfat al-Mujāhidīn* gives scope for research on many points. The details furnished by the book on a number of leading events have to be examined carefully whether they could stand the testimony of authenticated works published since the days of Shaykh Zainuddin. The introduction of Islam in the west coast, the conversion of one of the Hindu kings of Malabar to Islam, the various activities of the Portuguese in Southern India in the sixteenth century and such other information could not but evoke the interest of historians. While the particulars about seaports in the Indian peninsula attract geographers, the words like *Malībār, Ma'bar, Marakār and Sāmurī* will not fail to rouse philologists. It is hoped that the subject matter contained in the book will, by provoking criticism and stimulating research, serve to advance and extend our knowledge.

In conclusion, it gives me great pleasure to express my thanks to my affectionate friend Mr. M. Abdul Haq, M.A.,

D.Phil (Oxon), Professor of Arabic, and Principal, Government Muhammadan College, Mount Road, who has been kind enough to carefully read with me all the pages of the translation and make helpful suggestions.

S. Muhammad Husayn Nainar
University Buildings,
January 15, 1942.

Tuḥfat al-Mujāhidīn

Introduction

In the name of Allah, most Gracious, most Merciful.

All praises are due to Allah Who made the religion of Islam superior to all other religions and raised its adherents in dignity by stages over time. May Allah's blessings and peace be on His Messenger who paved the path to the religion of truth! And may His blessings and peace be on his family,[1] on his descendants and his Companions till the Judgement Day.

Allah, exalted be He, has bestowed on man not only his provision for his physical needs, but also His other most important blessings to man, ie., intelligence, judgement and discretion. Also He explained to man the way of achieving supreme felicity in life. To this end, He sent innumerable messengers to mankind—messengers who were the great leaders and guides, harbingers of glad tidings and warners, and who guided the people to the true knowledge about Allah.

Allah has conferred on us Muslims a special honour that other communities do not enjoy. That is, they have been exalted by being the community of Muḥammad (s), the noblest of His creation. He raised them above all other communities for this reason.[2] Allah says: "You are the best community that has been raised up for mankind."[3]

The Prophet (s) said: "I am the leader of the children of Adam. And it is not that I am saying this out of pride."[4] That

Prophet Muḥammad (s) is the leader of all children of Adam means he is uniquely superior to all of them. The superiority of the community is the natural corollary of the superiority of the Prophet (s). That is why Muslims are, as a community, superior to the rest.

Imām Aḥmad (r)[5] reports quoting Miqdād (r),[6] a companion of the Prophet (s): The Prophet (s) said: "Allah will not leave out any mansion or hut on earth without causing the message (*kalimah*) of Islam enter it either with the glory of the honoured, or with baseness of the mean. Either Allah will exalt them and bring them within its fold or demean them and make them submit to it."[7] I say religion, the whole of it, is for Allah.

Now it is a well known fact that Allah, glory be to Him and exalted be He, made the faith of Islam spread to most of the inhabited regions of the earth; in many countries by swords and force[8] and in some just by preaching. But Allah has been gracious to the people of Malabar in Hind in making them accept the faith of Islam willingly, not out of fear or compulsion.[9] This happened as follows:

A party of foreign Muslims entered some of the seaports of Malabar and settled there. In course of time, the inhabitants of these towns began to embrace Islam day by day. Before long, Islam spread all over the region at great pace and the Muslim population began to grow, and soon in the cities of Malabar heralded the settlement of Muslims in big numbers. In those days, they did not face any kind of opposition or oppression from the non-Muslim rulers who were then in power. As for these rulers, they continued to live adhering fully to their own ancient religion and its rites and practices.[10]

Thus Muslims continued to live in peace and prosperity by the boundless grace and blessings of Allah. But this condition did not last for long. The Muslims began to deviate into sinful living, forgetting the blessings of Allah and disobeying Him, and then Allah sent the cruel and wicked Portuguese Europeans to dominate over them.[11]

The Portuguese invaded the Muslim abodes and subjected them to all kinds of oppressions. The abominable atrocities and cruelties the Portuguese openly unleashed on the Muslims were countless. This Portuguese reign lasted for more than eighty years.[12] By that time, the condition of the Muslims had become extremely pathetic. They had become impoverished, weak and powerless. They could not find a way to get out of this wretched hole. And the militarily and economically powerful Muslim Sultans and Emirs reigning elsewhere did not come forward to rescue the Malabar Muslims from the calamity that had befallen on them. The reason was that these Sultans and Emirs, having little interest in religion and who loved this transient world more than the Next, would not struggle (*jihād*) in the path of Allah and spend their wealth in His cause.

I have undertaken the composition of this book in these circumstances. I have composed this with the intention of giving inspiration to the believers to wage war (*jihād*) against the cross-worshipping[13] Portuguese. The occasion for this effort is the fact that waging a holy war has become an obligation of all individual Muslims as the Portuguese had invaded and occupied the Muslim abodes. They killed innumerable Muslims. Those who were caught, bound and confined were countless in number. Many were forcefully converted to Christianity. Kidnapping Muslim women and raping them in custody to produce Christian children was rampant. Their intention behind these deeds was to prepare these children to harass and fight the Muslims when they are grown up.

I have entitled this book *"Tuḥfat al-Mujāhidīn fī baʿḍ Akhbār al-Burtughāliyyīn"*[a] (Tribute to the holy warriors in respect of a brief account of the Portuguese). I have narrated in it some of the cruelties done by the Portuguese against the faith of Islam in the land of Malabar; besides, it tells about the history of the advent and spread of Islam in Malabar, brief account of the laws pertaining to *jihād*, the great reward for it and the importance given to it in the Qur'an and the Prophetic Traditions (Ḥadīth)[b]; and the strange customs and practices of the Hindus in Malabar.

I dedicate this book to the noblest and the most respected of all rulers, one who takes delight in the struggle against disbelievers and regards fighting to uphold the divine word as a great honour. He sets his mind towards the service of the servants of Allah. His lofty courage disposes him to destroy the enemies of Allah. He is the reviver of the Faith, eradicating heresy and error from the territories of Allah. His main purpose is to love the learned, and to help the strangers and weak. He is a great ruler, whom the days and nights have refined, notwithstanding his young age; he is the possessor of eternal glory, in spite of great jealousies of his enemies. The noble acts of his generosity have covered the whole of the earth, and the character of his good deeds has permeated through all the quarters of the universe. The necks of the mighty bow down

---

a. The meaning of the title is: "A gratuitous gift to the holy warriors in respect of a brief account of the Portuguese."

b. During the life-time of Prophet Muḥammad (peace be on him) it was the custom that when two Muslims met, one should ask for news (*ḥadīth*) and the other should relate a saying or anecdote of the Prophet. After his demise this custom continued and the name 'Ḥadīth'—which primarily denoted a narrative or a report—has come to mean, in the Islamic theological usage, the records of the sayings and doings of the Prophet, and is translated in English as the Traditions.

before him; the nobles from the Arabs and non-Arabs submit to his authority. He is a noble sovereign, whose palms shower rain of gems upon the learned who come from distant lands; a gentle king whose kindness elevates the dignity of the noble men who preceded him. He is a ruler who meets with victory and success, and takes delights in pure and sincere deeds, and exploits which are counted in all assemblies and towns, while the annals of his generosity spread in all climes. He endeavours to root out the heretics and to extirpate the wrong doers. He spreads the banner of justice and mercy and stretches out his hand of benevolence and favour. Such is the mighty, victorious and compassionate Sultan, Sultan Ali Adil Shah.[14] May Allah exalt and strengthen the foundation of the Faith by means of his power. May he subdue the impious with his blaze and disperse their parties. May his kingdom extend over the east and the west; may he exercise his authority over land and sea and over the Arabs and non-Arabs; for he is the leader to whose noble qualities the east and the west have given testimony, and in whose service men and *jinns*[15] are diligent. Lover for men of knowledge and godliness is his innate nature; his exaltation of their ranks and respect for their words are as stated in the Law. May Allah grant perpetuity to his kindness and justice in the universe and enable him to pour on the people of the world his generosity and benevolence with the help of Muḥammad and his posterity.

This book consists of four sections and the fourth section has been divided into fourteen chapters.

- Section one: A treatise on the necessity of *jihād* and instructions thereof.
- Section two: The history of the advent and spread of Islam in Malabar.

- Section three: Certain strange customs of the Hindus in Malabar.
- Section four: This section, divided into fourteen chapters, speaks about the advent of the Portuguese to Malabar and the atrocities that followed:
  - Chapter one: The advent of the Portuguese in Malabar; their enmity towards the Muslims and the Zamorin; their construction of forts in Kochi, Kannur, Kollam, and their capture of the Goa port.
  - Chapter two: The Portuguese atrocities in Malabar.
  - Chapter three: The Zamorin's treaty with the Portuguese and their construction of a fort in Calicut.
  - Chapter four: The rivalry between the Zamorin and the Portuguese and the Zamorin's capture of the Calicut fort.
  - Chapter five: The second treaty between the Zamorin and the Portuguese and the construction of a Portuguese fort in Chliyam.
  - Chapter six: the Zamorin's third treaty with the Portuguese.
  - Chapter seven: The treaty of the Sultan of Gujarat, Bahadur Shah bin Muẓaffar, with the Portuguese and the ceding of certain ports to Portuguese.
  - Chapter eight: The visit to Diu and the neighbouring places by Sulayman Bāshā, the viceroy of the Turkey Caliph Sulaymān Shāh in Egypt, and his return to Egypt without success.
  - Chapter nine: The fourth treaty between the Zamorin and the Portuguese.
  - Chapter ten: A new rift between the Zamorin and the Portuguese.

- Chapter eleven: The fifth treaty between the Zamorin and the Portuguese.
- Chapter twelve: The causes of the rift between the Zamorin and the Portuguese and the naval attack on the Portuguese.
- Chapter thirteen: The conquest of the Chaliyam fort and the regaining the dignity Islam and the Muslims.
- Chapter fourteen: The predicament of the Portuguese after their loss of the Chaliyam fort.

The Author

SECTION ONE

A Treatise on the Necessity of *Jihād* and Instructions thereof

now then: there are two sets of unbelievers.[1] One is the group that permanently dwells in their countries. *Jihād*[2] against them is a collective duty, that means if some among the Muslims discharge that responsibility, then, the rest of them will be released from that duty. If nobody undertakes to do it, the entire community will be held responsible for committing sin of negligence.[3]

The other set of unbelievers are those who invade Muslim territories as is the situation we are facing now. Engaging them in war in such circumstances is the responsibility of every able-bodied individual adult Muslim, male and female living in the city.[4] For this, no slave[5] has to wait for the permission of his master, nor a wife that of her husband, nor the borrower that of the lender and nor the children that of their parents. It is binding on all who are not entitled to *qaṣr* in prayer.[6] But it will be incumbent on others (who are entitled to *qaṣr* in prayer) if the number of fighters is not sufficient. (Here what is meant by a territory is the area considered essential for shortening the regular prayers during travels. And if they too fail, the responsibility will fall on the people beyond that territory, then to the next territory, and so on.)

The leader (*amīr*) of the Muslim forces has to discuss matters concerning war with his companions in the struggles.[7] Then he must get the forces ready in well-disciplined rows. Once the war is over, the task of accumulating the spoils of war[8] and its fair distribution is the responsibility of the leader or the commander. The commander is bound to give the spoils taken from the killed—such as his clothes, boots or foot gears, waist belt, purse and the money in it, bangles, arms and war weapons, riding animal, its saddle and harness string etc.—to the one who killed him. The remainder of the spoils of war is to be divided into five equal shares. One of these five shares is to be divided further into another five portions. Out of these five portions, one portion is to be used for the public welfare of the Muslims such as fortifying the boundaries of the country, building forts, bridges, mosques, and for paying the remunerations of the *qāḍīs* and *imāms*.[9] The second portion is to be distributed to the relatives of the Prophet (s), the descendants of Hāshim and Muṭṭalib.[10] The third, fourth and the fifth portions are to be set apart for the orphans, the poor, and the wayfarers.

The remaining four main shares shall belong to the fighters who were present all the time of the battle and were engaged in it.

It must be the practice of those who fight against the unbelievers that they must, before they commence fighting, to supplicate to Allah and beseech Him for victory. They must have *taqwā* (piety and fear of Allah) and must be entrusting everything in Him, exalted be He, always keeping His remembrance in mind. Verily it is Allah Who helps to realize all our aspirations and intentions. The fighters must beware of any kind of perfidy in the distribution of the spoils of war. This is something to be feared most, as this is a matter concerning which warnings of severe punishments have come.[11]

It is well known that the Muslims of Malabar do not have a leader who possesses power and can exercise authority over them and be mindful of their welfare. All of them are subjects of the rulers who are non-believers. Notwithstanding, they kept on fighting their foreign enemies who were trying to dominate over them. They have already spent their wealth to the extent of their means in the cause of this struggle, with the generous help from the Muslim-friendly Zamorin,[12] who has been generously spending his wealth from the beginning. Yet, the enemies have been able to cause the Muslims large scale loss of lives and to rout them out of their commercial and industrial enterprises and to destroy their houses, as a result of which they became weaker, their poverty and destitution became intense and they became helpless and powerless.

The Muslim Sultans and Emirs—may Allah heighten the glory of the helpful among them—did not take any interest in the affairs of the Muslims of Malabar, although *jihād* is an obligatory duty upon them. Whoever from among the Sultans comes forward with wealth and sufficient preparations to challenge these non-believers and drive them out of Malabar and liberate the ports they have occupied, he will be a fortunate man deserving Allah's help and support. For, he is, by doing this noble deed, fulfilling his moral responsibility of obeying Allah's command and, at the same time, doing a deed that will absolve all Muslims of a most grievous sin of negligence.[13] Thus he will earn the pleasure of Allah, His angels,[14] His messengers and those who are close to Him[15] and also the boundless praise from all the people of east and west. He will, further, be bestowed countless rewards in the Hereafter. The weak and the poor in the society and the other noble and pious slaves of Allah will pray sincerely for him. Besides being rewarded for struggling in the cause of Allah and spending one's wealth for it, he will be rewarded for liberating the oppressed from their miserable plight. Imām Muslim[16] has reported the Prophet (s) to have said: "If ever anybody relieves a believer of a distress in this world, Allah will relieve him of his grief on the Day of Judgement." If, therefore, such rewards awaits a Muslim for relieving a believer of a single grief, then, how great might be the reward awaiting him for relieving innumerable poor souls of their grave miseries by waging war in the cause of Allah! *Subḥānallāh*! None but Allah can evaluate and weigh it.

Allah, glory be to Him and exalted be He, has urged the Muslims to take up the struggle in the cause of the liberation of the oppressed. Allah says in the Qur'an: "And why should you not fight in the cause of Allah and of those who, being weak, are ill-treated (and oppressed)?—Men, women, and children, whose cry is: Our Lord, rescue us from this town whose people are oppressors; and raise for us from You one who will protect; and raise for us from You one who will help." (Qur'an 4:75)[17]

Besides this, there are many other verses in the Qur'an, and likewise in the sayings of the Prophet (s), that show the merits of *jihād*, of spending one's wealth in that cause of keeping guard of the Muslim forces, and of martyrdom. Here are a few:

"Fighting is prescribed for you, and you dislike it. But it is possible that you dislike a thing which is good for you, and that you love a thing which is bad for you. But Allah knows and you know not." (Qur'an, 2:216)[18]

"Allah has purchased of the believers their persons and their goods, for theirs is the (garden of paradise) in return—they fight in His cause, and slay and are slain—a promise binding on Him in truth, through the Torah, the Gospel, and the Qur'an; and who is more faithful to his covenant than Allah? Then rejoice in the bargain which you have concluded. That is the supreme achievement." (Qur'an, 9:111)[19]

"The parable of those who spend their substance in the way of Allah is that of a grain of corn: it grows seven ears, and each ear has a hundred grains. Allah gives manifold increase to whom He pleases; and Allah cares for all and He knows all things." (Qur'an, 2:261)[20]

"Think not of those who are slain in Allah's way as dead. Nay, they live, finding their sustenance in the presence of their Lord. They rejoice in the bounty provided by Allah: and with regard to those left behind, who have not yet joined them (in their bliss), the (martyrs) glory in the fact that on them is no fear, nor have they (cause to) grieve." (Qur'an, 3:169-170)[21]

Al-Bukhārī[22] (r) and Muslim (r), quoting Abū Hurayrah,[23] report in their *Ṣaḥīḥs*:[24] When asked about what is the best of deeds, the Prophet (s) replied: "Believe in Allah and His messenger." When asked what was after that, he said: "*Jihād* in the cause of Allah." "Then what?" they asked. "Hajj[a] accepted by God," he replied.[25]

Al-Bukhārī (r) and Muslim (r) report from Abū Hurayrah: The messenger of Allah said: "Those who set out for *jihād*[26] inspired by faith in Allah and His Messenger, have only to gain

---

a. Pilgrimage (Ḥajj, lit. setting out). In the technical sense it means: to set out for visiting the *Bayt Allāh* (House of Allah) in Makkah. The pilgrimage to Makkah is performed in the month of Dhū al-Ḥijjah, the twelfth month of the Muslim year. The ḥajj is the fifth pillar of the religion of Islam. It is an incumbent religious duty founded upon express injunctions of the Qur'an. This duty is incumbent on every Muslim, once in his life time, if he be an adult, free, sane, healthy and has sufficient money for the expenses of the journey and for the support of his family during his absence.

profits. He will have gained plenty of spoils of war, and in case he dies and does not come back, he can be sure of paradise."

According to another report from Abū Hurayrah (r), the Messenger of Allah (s) said: "I swear in the name of Him in Whose possession is my soul, had it not for my fear that my absence from the city might distress the believers and they might dislike continue living here in my absence—as I do not have anything with me to keep them persuaded to stay here—I would not have kept away from any of the expeditions in the cause of Allah. I further swear in the name of Him in Whose possession is my soul, I desire to be slain in the cause of Allah and brought back to life and then to be slain again, and then brought back to life, and then to be slain again."[27]

Another report from Abū Hurayrah (r) is as follows: The Prophet (s) said: "A *mujāhid* who goes forth to fight in the cause of Allah is like one who is perpetually standing in prayer, fasting and reciting the divine verses, until he returns from the battle."[28]

Abū Hurayrah (r) reports again: "The Messenger of Allah (s) said: Allah takes notice of every wound or injury caused to one in the struggle in the cause of Allah. The injured will appear on the day of resurrection with blood gushing forth from his injuries. The colour of his blood will be the colour of blood, but its odour that of musk."[29]

Anas (r)[30] reports the Messenger of Allah (s) said: "A dawn in the cause of Allah or a dusk in His cause is better than this world and all that is contained in it."[31]

Anas (r) reports further: "The Messenger of Allah (s) said: None of those admitted to the heaven would like to return to the earth, even if every valuable thing on earth is going to be his, except the martyr. He would aspire to return to this world, and thus be killed ten times. This is because he holds martyrdom so great."[32]

Jābir (r)[33] says: "On the day of the battle of Uḥud,[34] a man asked the Prophet (s): Where shall I be if I get killed in this battle? 'In the heaven,' he replied. As soon as that man heard this, he ran to the battle ground throwing away the date he had in his hand and fought fiercely until he was slain."

Sahl bin Sa'd (r)[35] reports the Prophet (s) to have said: "Keeping guard and vigil for one day against the enemy is better than this world and all the valuables it contains."[36]

Abū Mūsā (r)[37] reports: "Once a man came to the presence of the Prophet and asked: 'There are people who fight for achieving fame and wealth. Who is the one that fights in the cause of Allah?' The messenger of Allah (s) replied: 'The one who fights for holding the words of Allah high'."[38]

Abū Sa'īd al-Khudrī (r)[39] says: The Prophet (s) said: "The believer who fights in the cause of Allah trusting his life and wealth with Allah is best of mankind."[40]

On the authority of Abū Hurayrah (r), al-Bukhārī (r) reports: "The Messenger of Allah (s) said: Allah has set apart a hundred grades of distinction in heaven for those who fight in His cause. The distance between one grade and the other is the distance between the heaven and earth. When you ask Allah, ask for *Firdaws*. It is in the centre of paradise and most grand. The throne of Allah, the most merciful, is above it. From it spring the rivers of paradise."[41]

Abū 'Abs (r)[42] says: The Prophet (s) has said: "The fire of Hell will not touch the one whose feet were soiled with dust in the cause of Allah."[43]

Abū Qays (r)[44] reports that he heard Sa'd (r) saying: "I am the first among the Arabs to shoot an arrow in the cause of Allah. We were fighting together in the company of the Messenger of Allah (s). Then, as we did not have anything else to eat, we were feeding ourselves on leaves of trees. Therefore, our excrement looked like the excrement of camels and sheep."[45]

Abū Hurayrah (r) relates: "The Prophet (s) has said: He who shall engage his horse in the way of Allah with faith in Him and belief in His promise, the food and drink he gives to the horse and its excrement will all weigh in his favour in the Balance on the Day of Resurrection."[46]

Quoting Abū Hurayrah (r), Muslim (r) reports: "The Prophet said: If ever any body dies without ever fighting, without even ever thinking about it in his mind, his death will be a death of some kind of hypocrisy."[47]

Abū Hurayrah (r) reports again: The Prophet (s) has said: "A non-believer and his slayer in battle will not come together in hell."[48]

Abū Hurayrah (r) reports further: The Prophet (s) has said: "For anyone the best of vocation in life is that he holds the harness of a horse in his hands in the cause of Allah; he rushes to every noisy and tumultuous spot on his horse yearning for death or meaning to kill; or that of one who lives on this hill or valley grazing his sheep, performing the prayers regularly and giving *zakāh* (obligatory charity) to those who are eligible for it and thus remains in the worship of Allah until his death. Such people will be successful."[49]

Jābir bin Samurah (r)[50] reports: The Prophet (s) has said: "This religion will surely survive. There will always be a group among Muslims to fight for it until the last day."[51]

Salmān al-Fārisī (r)[52] said that he heard the Prophet (s) say: "Keeping vigil against the enemies one whole night and one whole day is greater in virtue than fasting for a month and being in prayer all night. If he gets killed while doing so, the reward and grade of distinction he gets will be the same as what he might have got for carrying out his mission to full success. His provisions are certain and he will be free from all miseries."[53]

'Uqbah bin 'Āmir (r)[54] reports: Once I heard the Prophet (s) say from the pulpit, "Make as much preparations as you can against your enemies. Hark, archery is power, archery is power, archery is power." In another place, 'Uqbah bin 'Āmir reports the Prophet (s) to have said: "One who learned archery and later abandoned it is not one of us."[55]

Abū Mas'ūd al-Anṣārī (r)[56] reports: Once a man came to the Prophet with a harnessed mare and said: 'I submit this in the cause of Allah.' The Prophet (s) told him: 'For this, you will get seven hundred mares harnessed on the Day of Resurrection.'[57]

Masrūq (r)[58] relates: We asked 'Abdullah bin Mas'ūd (r)[59] about the following verse of the Qur'an: "Think not of those who are slain in Allah's way as dead. Nay, they live, finding their sustenance in the presence of their Lord. They rejoice in the bounty provided by Allah: and with regard to those left behind, who have not yet joined them (in their bliss), the (martyrs) glory in the fact that on them is no fear, nor have they (cause to) grieve." 'Abdullah bin Mas'ūd (r) explained it as follows from what he learned from the Prophet (s): "The souls of those who died in the cause of Allah are cheerfully flying and fluttering about in the Heaven taking the shape of green-coloured birds. Some lamps are hung down from the divine throne for them. They flock together around those lamps. Allah appears before them and asks whether they do wish anything. They reply: 'What else do we wish for? We are already in the blissful Heaven and go about wherever we choose.' They were asked this question three times. Thus finally perceiving that Allah will not let them go without asking for a favour, they pray: 'O Lord! We wish our souls were back to our bodies, so that we get killed once more in Your cause.' Since they did not have any other wish, Allah disappears."[60]

'Abdullah bin 'Amr bin al-'Āṣ (r)[61] reports: The Prophet has said: "Death in the cause of Allah will redeem everything except debt."[62]

Anas (r) gives an account of the scene of the Prophet (s) and his companions confronting the polytheists in Badr:[63] The Prophet told his companions: "Rise to the heaven! It's as wide as the skies and the earth."[64] 'Bravo! Bravo!' 'Umayr bin al-Hamām (r) cried out.

"'What makes you shout like that?,' the Prophet (s) asked.

"'O Messenger of Allah, by Allah! I say so for no other reason than my hope of being one of the dwellers of paradise!' he said. 'Yes, certainly you are already one of them,' the Prophet replied. He has been eating dates from his little quiver. As soon as he heard these words of the Prophet (s), he threw aside all his dates, saying: 'If I have life until I finish eating this date, for me that much time is too long a time of life!' Thus he fought against the enemies and was killed."[65]

Al-Tirmidhī (r) and Abū Dāwūd (r) report from Fuḍālah bin 'Ubayd (r)[66]: The Prophet (s) said: "The deeds of every individual will be terminated by his death except in the case of one who has been keeping vigil against the enemies in the cause of Allah and is killed. His deeds will keep growing until the final day. He will be safe from all the miseries of the grave too."

Quoting Abū Umāmah (r)[67], Abū Dāwūd (r) reports: The Prophet (s) has said: "If ever there is a man who does not fight in a battle or help a fighter to get ready for a struggle, or co-operate in the effort, or at least do the best service to the family of a fighter in his absence, divine wrath will come upon him in this world itself before the Day of Resurrection."[68]

'Imrān bin Ḥuṣayn (r)[69] reports: The Prophet has said: "I will always have a group of followers who fight for the truth and remain brave and stern before the enemies, until al-Dajjāl is killed in the end."[70]

Al-Tirmidhī (r) quotes Ibn 'Abbās (r)[71]: The Prophet (s) has said: "The hell-fire will not touch two kinds of eyes. The eyes that weep out of fear of Allah and the eyes that keep vigil in the cause of Allah."[72]

Abū Hurayrah (r) reports: Once one of the Companions[73], while travelling along a mountain valley, came across a river with crystal clear water flowing in it. Allured by that, he wished to settle down in that locality, away from his people. When told about this, the Prophet (s) responded: "Nay, the reward and grade of a man who sets out for *jihād* in the cause of Allah is greater than what a man can achieve by performing prayers at home for seventy years. Don't you wish Allah pardons your sins and enters you to the heaven? Fight in the cause of Allah! One who has fought in the way of Allah as much time as is required for a camel to secrete milk after having been milked once, can be assured of entering the heaven?"[74]

Al-Tirmidhī (r) and al-Nasā'ī (r) report, on the authority of Abū Hurayrah (r): The Prophet has said: "The martyr does not experience pangs of death but as light as that of a bite."[75]

Khuraym bin Fātik (r)[76] reports: The Prophet (s) has said: "Whoever spends his wealth in the cause of Allah will find it accounted with Allah seven hundred times."[77]

Ibn Mājah (r) records quoting from 'Alī (r),[78] Abū al-Dardā' (r),[79] Abū Hurayrah (r), Abū Umāmah (r), 'Abdullah bin 'Umar (r),[80] Jābir bin 'Abdullah (r) and 'Imrān bin Ḥuṣayn (r): The Prophet (s) has said: "Whoever is staying at home having donated his wealth for the struggle in the cause of Allah, will get seven hundred fold in return for every dirham he has spent. Whoever takes part in the struggle, besides spending his wealth in the cause of Allah, will get seven hundred thousand fold for every dirham." Then the Prophet (s) read out this verse from the Qur'an: "Allah gives manifold increase to whom He pleases; and Allah cares for all and He knows all things." (Qur'an, 2:261)[81]

Abū Dāwūd reports quoting Ibn 'Abbās: The Prophet (s) advised his companions, "Allah lets the souls of your brothers martyred in the battle of Uḥud take the shape of green birds. They cheerfully flutter about and fly over the rivers of the heaven and eat the fruits there and take rest near the golden lamps hung down from beneath the divine throne. When they came to realise the taste of the food and the drinks there, and the comfort of their resting place, they spoke to each other: 'Who will let our brothers know about our being in the heaven that they may not shun the heaven and feel frightened of the struggle?' Allah replied: 'I will do it for you.' It was following this that He revealed the Qur'anic verse beginning: 'Think not of those who are slain in Allah's way as dead…'."[82]

Al-Ḥākim (r)[83] reports, quoting from Abū Mūsā al-Ash'arī (r), that the Messenger of Allah (s) has said that the heaven is under the shadow of the sword.[84]

Anas (r) reports from Ibn Mājah (r): the Messenger of Allah (s) has said: "The dust and soil that gathers on the body of one who travels for *jihād* in the cause of Allah will turn into musk on the Day of Resurrection."

Al-Ṭabarānī (r)[85] writes in *al-Kabīr* quoting Ibn 'Umar (r): The Prophet (s) has said: "Who breaks his head in the cause of Allah will be forgiven for whatever his previous sins."

Wā'ilah (r)[86] says: The Prophet (s) said: "Whoever did not get a chance to fight together with me shall fight at sea."[87]

Al-Daylamī (r)[88] writes in *Musnad al-Firdaws* quoting Abū Hurayrah (r) that the Prophet (s) said: "Fighting in the cause of Allah for one hour is greater in virtue than performing ḥajj fifteen times."

The situation of one who takes part in the holy struggle is much different from that of a ḥajj pilgrim. The warrior in the cause of Allah is setting out on a journey to Allah renouncing his self and his wealth. The benefit of his engaging in war is for the society as a whole. This is how one hour fighting in the cause of Allah becomes more virtuous than performing ḥajj fifteen times.

Section Two

History of the Advent and Spread of Islam in Malabar

party of Jews and Christians with their families arrived in a big ship in Kodungallur, the port city of Malabar.[1] Kodungallur was then also the capital city of the king. They secured from the king grants of lands, plantations and houses and thus they settled there.

Some years later, there arrived at Kodungallur a party of Muslims, who were poor, with a *shaykh*. They were on their way to visit the footprint of our father Adam in Ceylon.[2] When the king heard about their arrival, he sent for them, entertained them, and treated them hospitably. The leader of the group, the *shaykh*, informed the king about Prophet Muḥammad (s) and the religion of Islam. They also talked about the miraculous incident of the splitting of the moon.[3] Allah, glory be to Him and exalted be He, caused to enter in his mind the truth of the Prophet's mission. He heartily acknowledged him and his love for the Prophet took possession of his heart. He asked the *shaykh* and his companions to call on him on their return journey from their visit to the footprint of Adam for the reason he might go with them. He commanded the *shaykh* to keep this very confidential and not to let anyone in Malabar know about his secret intention.

Thus, on their return journey from Ceylon, they called on the king. The king asked the *shaykh* to arrange, without any one's knowledge, the ship and other things necessary for his journey with them.

There were laying in the port several ships belonging to foreign traders. The *shaykh* requested the owner of one of the ships to let him and a group of poor people travel on board his ship. The ship owner readily, and with pleasure, agreed.

As the day fixed for the voyage neared, the king gave orders to the effect that none of his family or ministers shall come to visit him for seven days. Then he set himself dividing his kingdom into several provinces and set clear boundaries for each of them; then appointing governors for each province and wrote out detailed instructions defining the limits of territories of each so that one might not encroach upon the limits specified for the other. This incident is quite well-known among the Hindus in Malabar.[4] He was the sovereign monarch of the whole territory of Malabar with Kumhuri (Kanyakumari) as its boundary in the south and Kanjarakut (Kasaragod) in the north.[5]

Then king embarked with the *shaykh* and his people during night time and reached Pantalayani[6] where they landed and stayed for a day and night. Thence they proceeded to Darmadam[7] where they stayed three days. Then they set sail till they reached Shuhr[a] (Shahar al-Mukalla),[8] where the king stayed for several days with the *shaykh* and his people. There, another party of travellers joined them. It was a group bound for Malabar with the mission of preaching Islam and constructing mosques and establishing regular prayers there.[9]

---

a. From the way it is mentioned in the book it appears to be the name of a particular place rather than the Arabian Court as Rowlandson would have it. *The Keralolpatti* says that Cheraman Perumal landed at the port of Sahar Mukhal on the Arabian coast. (Padmanabha Menon, *History of Kerala*, Vol. I, p. 433). It is possible that both refer to the same place.

The King fell ill while staying in Shahar al-Mukalla. Realising that illness was getting worse and his recovery very remote, the king beckoned to his side Sharaf bin Mālik, a member of the group bound for Malabar, and Mālik bin Dīnār, his half brother from his mother's side and others, and said: "Do not give up the idea of travelling to India even if I die of this illness."

"We do not know anything about your country, where it is and how vast it is. We had intended to come with you," was their reply to the king. Hearing this, the king thought for a while and then gave them a letter in Malayalam. The letter contained detailed information about his kingdom, its provinces, the members of his family, and the names and other details of the rest of the kings in Malabar. The king further advised them to go ashore anywhere off Kodungallur, Darmadam, Pantalayani or Kollam. He further instructed them, specifically, not to disclose to anybody in Malabar anything about his serious illness or about his death in case it so happens.[10]

Before long, the king passed away. May the Almighty Allah shower on him His abundant blessings![11]

A few years later, the party consisting of Sharaf bin Mālik, Mālik bin Dīnār, and Mālik bin Ḥabīb, his wife Qamariyyah, their children and friends set out on their voyage to Malabar. They reached the coast of Kodungallur after several days of voyage.[12] They handed the letter the king had given them to the then ruler of the place.[13] They did not disclose the news of the king's death to them. Obliging the directions in the letter, the ruler of the place gave lands and estates for their use. Following this, they settled down and built a mosque there.[14]

Mālik bin Dīnār decided to settle down in Kodungallur and assigned Mālik bin Ḥabīb, his nephew, to the rest of the regions of Malabar to build mosques and preach Islam.[15] Thus Mālik bin Ḥabīb, taking all his belongings, moved to Kollam with his wife and some of his children. He built a mosque in Kollam, and settled down his wife and children there. Leaving them behind there, he moved further to Ezhimala,[16] and built a mosque there, too. Then he reached Barkur,[17] Mangalore,[18] and Kasaragod[19] and built mosques in all these places. Having accomplished all these, he returned to Ezhimala and stayed there for three months. Then, he visited Sreekandapuram, Darmadam, Pantalayani, and Chaliyam[20] and built mosques in all these places. He stayed in Chaliyam for five months. Then he went back to Kodungallur and stayed with his uncle Mālik bin Dīnār. In the meanwhile he made a second trip visiting all the mosques he had built in various parts of Malabar and performed prayers in all of them. Praising Allah and expressing deep gratitude to Him he returned overjoyed to find the divine light of Islam having taken over so much space in the abysmal darkness of disbelief.

Then Mālik bin Dīnār and Mālik bin Ḥabīb with their friends and servants went to Kollam. From there, Mālik bin Dīnār and a few others set sail to Shahar al-Mukalla, and the rest of them settled in Kollam. In Shahar al-Mukalla, he visited the tomb of the deceased king, and then travelled to Khurasan,[21] where he eventually died. Mālik bin Ḥabīb, after making arrangements for some of his children to settle in Kollam, returned to Kodungallur with his wife. It was while in Kodungallur that he and his wife breathed their last.[22]

This is the history of the advent and spread of Islam in Malabar. We do not have any clear evidence to say for sure which year this happened. The majority opinion is that it happened in 200 AH. However, the general impression with the Muslims in Malabar is that the aforesaid king's conversion to Islam took place during the time of the Prophet (s). They believe that the king one night saw in person the splitting of the moon, following which he set out to meet the Prophet (s) and after meeting the Prophet (s), he died at Shahar al-Mukalla on his way back to Malabar with a group of Muslims. There is but little truth in this.[23]

It is a widely accepted belief today that the king's grave is not in Shahar al-Mukalla, but at Ẓāfar in Yemen and that this grave known as Sāmurī is looked upon as a holy place by the local people.[24]

The story of the king's disappearance is well-known among all people in Malabar, Muslims and Hindus. The Hindus, however, say that the king ascended to the sky and that he will come down one day. It is based on this belief that a pair of wooden sandals and a pitcher of water are kept ready, with lit lamps and decorations, at a particular location in Kodungallur on a certain night.

It is also well known among them that the king divided and distributed his territory and power; and it is said that the Zamorin, who later became the first king of Calicut, did not get any share as he was not present there at the time of the partition. When he turned up late, the king gave him his sword[a] and said:

---

a. According to the local tradition, when Cheraman Perumal retired in his old age he assigned a small area to his nephew and gave him a sword instructing him to "kill and annex". This nephew later on became famous as the Zamorin of Calicut. He kept the sword given by his uncle with great veneration. This sword was burnt to cinders when the Dutch sacked the temporary residence of the Zamorin at Tiruvaneikkulam in 1671 AD. The sword which the Zamorin has now in his possession with an inscription on it in Malayalam characters,

"Grab power fighting with this."[25] Thus the Zamorin fought and took possession of Calicut.

After some time, Muslims began to settle down there. Traders and craftsmen flocked there from various regions. Thus Calicut was transformed into a big city, where, with prospering trade and job opportunities, various kinds of people, Muslims as well as unbelievers, collected. The Zamorin, thus, became more influential and powerful than the rest of the rulers in Malabar.

All the rulers of Malabar are Hindus. There are some who are powerful and some comparatively weak. But the strong, as a matter of fact, will not attack or occupy the territory of the weak. This might be the result of the final advice of their king who embraced Islam and of his supplications to this effect to God. This was also because of the blessings of the Prophet (s) and the religion of Islam he founded.

There are in Malabar chieftains whose territories do not exceed one parasang (about three and a half square miles or less than that), while others have powers over more extensive territories. Of these some have at their command one hundred soldiers or less, or two hundred to three hundred, thousand, five thousand, ten thousand, thirty thousand, hundred thousand and more, and so on. Some territories join in league and are governed by two or three persons together. And of them some have greater power and bigger army. Quarrels and skirmishes take place occasionally among them, but this does not affect their coalition rule.

Of all the kings in Malabar, Tiruwadi,[26] the ruler of the territories between Kollam and Kanyakumari, has the largest number of troops. Next to him comes Kolattiri, the ruler of

---

was made subsequently. See Logan, *Malabar Manual*, for a picture of the same.

Ezhimala, Sreekandapuram, Kannur, Edakkad, Darmadam and other cities.[27] But the Zamorin enjoyed greater power and reputation than the rest. He is quite influential among the rest of the kings. The Zamorin came to enjoy this distinction on account of the greatness of Islam. He treats the Muslims, especially the foreign Muslims, with great affection and respect. However, the Hindus believe this to be on account of the greatness of the sword he got from the aforesaid king. They claim the sword which is kept preserved in the Zamorin's palace is the same sword. They have great adoration and respect towards that sword. When the Zamorin goes forth to battle or to a big assembly, a servant carrying this sword walks in front.[28]

Whenever the Zamorin fights for one reason or other against a weak ruler and subdues him, the tradition is for that ruler to give the Zamorin an annual tribute or, at times, his kingdom altogether.[a] If the subdued king does not give, he would not be forced to do so though a long time may lapse in waiting. This is because people of Malabar honour and cherish the traditions and customs dearly. They do not violate it deliberately, except some unintentional violations which take place rarely. But the kings other than the Zamorin do not follow this tradition. Only thing they can do is to fight to destroy the kingdom of the opponent during the war and kill people if they can.

---

a. This is quite in accordance with the practice of the kings of ancient India. The conqueror was content if the vanquished king acknowledged his suzerainty and agreed to pay an annual tribute. The ancient kings of India were not particular about the confiscation of the conquered country and the dethronement of the defeated chief.

SECTION THREE

Certain Strange Customs of the Hindus in Malabar

Know then: some very strange and unique customs are prevalent among the Hindus in Malabar, such as not seen anywhere else in the world.

If a ruler is killed in a battle, all his troops will come together to fight against his adversary, his forces and his country, till they have killed them all or laid desolate the entire land of his enemy.[a] They will not turn back until and unless either one of these happens. Therefore, both sides dread the idea of killing the leader of the forces of the other side. This has been one of their ancient customs, although not so much in vogue in these days.[1]

The rulers of Malabar are mainly of two groups: supporters of the Zamorin and supporters of the king of Kochi. Normally they do not change sides except on some temporary issues. When the issue is settled the ruler who changed his side will go back to his original side.

People of Malabar are never treacherous in their wars. When war was found unavoidable, they fixed a date for it in advance. Nobody acts against the terms of this mutual agreement. Deceit in this respect is looked upon as undignified and base.

Year long abstinence is observed by the Brahmins, the carpenters and others of the patriarchal system to mourn the

---

a. For details given by Arab writers on the subject see my book, *Arabs' Knowledge of Southern India*, pp. 106-7.

death of elder members of the clan such as father, mother or elder brother; and for the Nairs, who are of the matriarchal system, abstinence is on the death of mother, uncle and elder brother. During the period of abstinence, it is taboo for them to trim their hair or nails, eat fish or meat, chew betel leaves, or have intercourse with women. They never deviate from such practice as they believe that the deceased are blessed by their doing so.

In the matriarchal communities like the Nairs, the deceased will be inherited by his/her brothers on the mother side, sisters' children, aunts and other relatives of his or her mother. Inheritance right, weather it is the right to property or to the political power of kingship, does not go to one's children, but to one's nieces and nephews. This custom[a] of denying inheritance right to male children, following the Hindu practice, has crept into most families of the Muslim community in Kannur and the neighbouring places. They read the Qur'an; they learn it by heart; they recite it beautifully; they acquire religious learning; they perform prayers and other forms of worship; yet, it is extremely strange and surprising that this custom prevails among them.[2]

But the right for inheritance of the deceased father is for his children in the Brahmin, the goldsmith, the carpenter, the blacksmith, the Thiyya and the fishermen communities. Marriage among these communities has certain rules and customs to be followed. But marriage among the Nairs is only a man tying a string of thread around the neck of a woman.[3] After that, things are the same as before. For her, practically there is no difference between the one who has tied the string around her neck and the others.[4]

---

a. This is a reference to the system of *Marumakkattayam* obtaining in Malabar.

In the Brahmin community, if there are many brothers in a family, only the eldest ever takes a wife in marriage. The next gets married only when the eldest is not likely to have an issue. This is to avoid quarrels and disputes over inheritance when the number of heirs multiplies. The younger brothers, as a rule, engage in illicit sexual relationship with Nair women. The children born of them by Nair women thus are not entitled to inherit their father's wealth.

The women of the Nair community as well as those communities close to it in hierarchy usually have two or four or sometimes more husbands, each in turn passing the night just as a Muslim husband divides his night among his wives. Enmity or ill-will does not come into their mind on that account.

The practice among the communities, such as carpenters, Karuvas and goldsmiths, is for all brothers to marry just one woman. All husbands ought to be, if not brothers, at least of the same family. This custom is followed strictly to avoid disputes over inheritance of properties or at least to minimise it.[5]

The Hindus of Malabar expose their bodies. They usually wear a short piece of cloth that covers from their waist to just below their knees and keep the rest of the body bare. All are alike in this regard: men and women, elders and youngsters, the rich and the poor, the kings and the subjects, all alike! Generally women will appear before anybody. However, the Brahmin women, as a rule, remain indoors.[6] They do not go out like the rest of the women.[7] Nairs let their women adorn themselves with expensive clothes and ornaments and attend big festivals so that their beauty is seen and enjoyed by men.

In Malabar, the eldest, even though senior by a minute, succeeds to the throne, no matter whether he is blind, stupid or disabled or be from sons of maternal aunts. However, nothing is so far heard about anybody killing a senior person to grab power in haste.

The practice of adopting from another clan, when it is the case that there is very few or none to inherit a family property or kingdom, is prevalent among the people in Malabar. Adoption is not always of children. Sometimes even adults are adopted. The adopted person is treated like a real son, nephew or brother and is given inheritance, power and position, without discrimination. This custom of adoption is prevalent among all sections of the Hindu society, among the rulers and common people, among the high and the low. Thus, through this custom, the line of succession is never broken.

The Hindus of Malabar loyally maintain their caste system. Because of this, they encounter many difficulties. Yet, they do not attempt to violate the norms of the caste system or to do away with the system. The Hindus here belong to many different castes. There are among them high castes, low castes and castes of other degrees in between. A bath is obligatory on high cast Hindu in the event of any physical contact with the members of the low castes or they happen to be together within the boundaries and limits prescribed for intercourse. It is taboo to take food before the compulsory bath that washes him clean. If he takes food before doing so, he will be degraded from his rank and will result in his being excommunicated. In that case, he will have no option other than leave the place and go to a remote and unknown place, where he will not be recognized, to spend the remainder of his life. Else, the local ruler will seize him and sell him to one of the inferior rank, whether the purchaser is a boy or a woman. Or else, he comes to us and embraces Islam, or becomes a yogi or turns a Christian. The same fate awaits a high caste member if he or she eats the food prepared by the low caste.

Those who wear Poonool are considered of high castes.[a] They usually wear a string suspended from their shoulders. There are further hierarchical divisions within them: low, higher and highest. The highest among the wearers of Poonool are the Nambootiris.[8]

After the Poonool wearers comes Nair caste. This caste, known for their physical strength and larger in numbers, is the martial caste of Malabar. They too have many subdivisions, high, middle and low ranks.[9]

The Thiyyas are below the Nairs in the caste hierarchy. Their customary job is climbing the coconut trees to extract a kind of juice from them. This liquid could be fermented to make toddy or used for making a sort of sugar (*shakkra*).

The carpenters, the Karuvas, the goldsmiths and the fishermen are below the Thiyyas on the caste ladder. There are several castes below these castes. They work as ploughmen and in other works related to farming. There are sub-castes even in all these castes.[b]

If a woman of a higher caste, on certain particular nights of the year, happens to be hit with a stone or something else from the hands of a man of inferior caste and she was not at that time accompanied by any man, she will be turned out of her caste. In such circumstances, she has no alternative other than embracing

---

a. The classification of the wearers of thread into three grades appears to be after the communities of Brahmans, Ksatriyas and Vaisyas who are all entitled to wear the sacred thread. Of them the Brahmans rank first, then come the Ksatriyas, and then the Vaisyas.
b. They were probably the ancestors of the Eluvas, Parayas and Pulayas of the modern day.

Islam, Christianity or become a yogi. Otherwise she will be sold by the local ruler.[10]

The same is the case when a person of the higher caste had sex with a person of the lower caste.[a] The man or the woman of the higher caste, in such cases, will become outcaste, and will have to accept any of the above mentioned fates and they will have no other alternative. But the case of the Poonool wearing Brahmins is different. They may have sex with the womenfolk of the Nair community. They will not become outcastes because of this, as this is an accepted custom. As was explained earlier, only the eldest of the sons of the Nambootiri families ever get married and the younger sons, as a rule, may keep company with Nair women.[11]

How many such detestable customs! Due to their ignorance and stupidity, they strictly follow these customs believing that it is their moral responsibility to uphold them. It was while they were living in these social conditions that the religion of Islam reached them by the grace of Allah. And this was also the main reason for their being easily attracted to Islam.

These issues are not, in fact, our subject. Only a digression so that certain information of great values the readers must know. Now we shall return to the subject of our narrative.

As told before, people of the coastal areas of Malabar began to sporadically embrace Islam as a result of the efforts of Sharaf bin Mālik, Mālik bin Dīnār, Ḥabīb bin Mālik and others by building mosques and propagating the message of Islam in these regions. Consequently, traders from many parts of the world kept coming to these places in large numbers. Thus places like Calicut, Weliancode, Tirurangadi, Tanur, Ponnani, Parappanan-

---

a. For details given by Arab writers on the subject see my book, *Arabs' Knowledge of Southern India*, p. 112.

gadi, Parawanna, the localities surrounding Chaliyam port, Kakkad, Tikkodi, other localities surrounding Pantalayani, Kannur, Edakkad, Tiruwangad, Mahe, Chemmanad, the localities surrounding Darmadam, on its south Walapttanam and Nadapuram, on the south of Kodungallur, Kochi, Vypeen, Pallippuram, and several other coastal areas became thickly populated and grew into towns with thriving trade and commerce, all because of Muslims. The Muslims and their trade prospered because of the great tolerance with which the rulers and their military, though they were Hindus, treated the Muslims. They were not Hindus only in name, but pious people who strictly observe their ancestral customs and rites in practice. Seldom did they do anything amiss so far as their religious rites were concerned. The Muslims then were, in fact, their subjects and not even accounted one tenth of the population. Yet, they did not treat the Muslims in any way hostile or unfriendly except on rare occasions.

Calicut was a big and well-known port in Malabar from very ancient times. But it began to decline and to lose its significance with the advent of the Portuguese to Malabar and the obstructions to trade journeys created by them.

Muslims throughout Malabar have no leader possessed of power to rule over them. But their rulers are Hindus, who exercise judicial authority and organize their affairs by enforcing payment of debt or fine if anyone is subjected to such payment. Notwithstanding these, Muslims enjoyed great respect and regard from the Hindu rulers. The main reason for this is that the construction and development of the country is taking place largely through the Muslims. Hence the rulers make it convenient for the Muslims to organize Friday congregation prayers (*jum'ah*) and the celebrations like 'Īd. The remuneration for the *mū'adhdhins* (those who call to prayer) and the *qāḍīs* (religious judges) are paid by the government. The government makes special arrangements for implementing among the Muslims their own religious rules and regulations. In greater part of Malabar, whoever neglects the *jum'ah* (the Friday congregation) is punished or made to pay a fine.

In the event of a Muslim committing a crime punishable with death, they carry out the sentence with the consent of the elders of the Muslim community, and the mortal remains of the man will be handed to the Muslims for burial. Afterwards, the body is given the ritualistic wash, prayers for the dead is performed and buried in the Muslim cemetery. But when a non-Muslim commits similar crime, they either kill him or gibbet him, and leave the body to be devoured by dogs and jackals.

The government exacts one-tenth of the profits of the traders. If they commit any offences liable to a fine, they will have to pay such fines. No land tax or harvest tax of any kind is imposed on farmers or land owners however much land they may have in their possession.

People of the other communities enter Muslim houses only after obtaining permission in advance. They will not enter their houses without permission for catching an accused hiding inside even he is wanted for a crime of murder. They ask the household only to force him out by leaving him to starve or by other means. In the case of Hindus embracing Islam, other Hindus do not, as a rule, put any impediments nor do they harm them by any means. On the other hand, they are customarily treated with respect along with the rest of the Muslims, even if they were of the lower caste. In the early days, Muslim traders raised funds collectively for helping those new converts to Islam.

Section Four

The Arrival of the Portuguese in Malabar and a Brief Account of Their Shameful Deeds

The Portuguese entry into Malabar; hostilities between them and the Zamorins; the erection of forts by them in Kochi, Kannur and Kollam, and their capture and occupation of the port of Goa

It was in the year 904 AH (1498 AD) the Portuguese made their first appearance in Malabar.[1] They arrived at Pantalayani in three ships.[2] By then the trade season through sea routes was almost over. From Pantalayani they moved to Calicut by land, stayed in that town for few months and returned to their homeland after collecting information about the conditions of Malabar. On this occasion, they did not engage themselves in any trade. The main purpose of their trip to Malabar, according to their own accounts, was to seek information about the pepper-land and to establish trade in that commodity, for at that time they were buying pepper from other traders who export pepper from Malabar.[3]

They came again after two years, this time in six ships. They landed at Calicut and engaged themselves in trade.

They approached the officers of the Zamorin with a request to stop the Muslims from their trade and trade voyages to Arabia, promising to pay double the loss the Zamorin might suffer by preventing Muslims in this respect. Then they began to encroach upon the rights of the Muslims in all directions. So the Zamorin gave orders to capture and kill the Portuguese invaders. Following this, about sixty or seventy of them were put to death. The rest took to their heels and sought refuge in their ships, and started firing from the ships to the shore. Those on the shore returned fire to the ships.

The Portuguese then moved to the Kochi port and made peace with the inhabitants of that town, and built a small fort and camped there. That was the first Portuguese fort built in India.[4] They demolished a mosque situated on the coast and built a church in its place, employing local people as labourers.

Then they arrived at Kannur, made peace with the people there, built a fort and engaged in trade.[5] Then they set sail to their homeland with their ships heavily laden with pepper and dried ginger. That was, after all, the main purpose of their coming here by undertaking such long journeys.

The Portuguese came again after a year, this time in four ships. Harbouring at Kochi and Kannur, they accumulated as much pepper and dried ginger as they wanted and returned home.[6] Two years after that they came again to Hind with twenty or twenty one or twenty two or eighteen ships, and having laden their ships with variety of merchandise besides pepper and dried ginger, they returned to their own country.[7] Thus their influence kept growing.

It was during this time the Zamorin attacked Kochi[a] and, according to his wont, caused heavy devastation and loss to

---

a. This took place in 1503; perhaps this was the second invasion in the same year.

them. In this encounter the Zamorin slew two or three of the Kochi chieftains and then returned to Calicut.

The Zamorin killed the chieftains because their alliance with the Portuguese had helped the nephews of the chieftains to usurp the throne of Kochi and the neighbouring places with the aid of Portuguese, contrary to the time-honoured custom of electing to the throne the senior-most man from among the relatives. Thus the Portuguese were treated with consideration and respect by the usurpers. The Portuguese in return helped them much in their wars and, in times of need, assisted them with money; and also set apart for them a tenth of their profits from trade. As a result the importance and influence of the Portuguese were increasing.

A year after the arrival of the twenty or so ships mentioned above, another party reached Hind in a fleet of ten ships. Seven of them were newly arriving ships whilst the other three were those of the earlier fleet of twenty one ships which had come the year before. As their passage had been hindered on their homeward journey, they joined and returned with the seven ships. On arrival at Kochi, the seven ships loaded with merchandise set out on their homeward voyage. The three ships remained in Kochi.

When the Zamorin came to know of the three Portuguese ships in Kochi, he set out to Kochi with an army of about 100,000 Nair soldiers accompanied by a good number of Muslim warriors to seize the ships. But the Zamorin and his forces could not enter Kochi. The Portuguese fought with cannon and arrows.[8] However, the Muslim fighters from Ponnani equipped themselves in three boats and fought the Portuguese. Some Muslims were martyred. The following day, Muslims from Ponnani and Weliancode in four boats and the Muslims from Pantalayani and Kakkad in three boats set out to the sea and fought the Portuguese a fierce battle. Muslims did not suffer any casualty on this occasion. The battle was indecisive because of the setting in of the rainy season. Therefore the Zamorin and his forces returned to Calicut safely. May Allah be praised.

Thus it became customary for the Portuguese to come with ships laden with people and cargoes and to return with pepper, dried ginger and several other produces, year after year. After the Portuguese settled in Kochi and Kannur and secured a firm footing there, the inhabitants of these towns with their dependents engaged themselves in sea voyages taking with them passes from the Portuguese to avoid risks. Each ship, however small, was issued with a pass, for which the Portuguese fixed a fee: at the time of the voyage the master of the ship took the pass on payment of the fee. The Portuguese impressed upon the people that the system of pass introduced by them was to their advantage and thus induced them to submit to it. Whenever the Portuguese fell in with a ship which did not possess their pass, they seized the ship, its crew and cargo. On account of this high-handedness, the Zamorin, his subjects and dependents were constantly fighting against the Portuguese.

The Zamorin spent a lot of his wealth in this war, and before long he and his subjects declined in strength. So the Zamorin dispatched letters to Muslim Sultans seeking help. They did not come forward to help him. But the Sultan of Jazrāt (Gujarat), Sultan Mahmud Shah, the father of esteemed Sultan Muzaffar Shah, and Adil Shah, the grandfather of the great Sultan Ali Adil Shah[9] (may Allah light their graves), gave orders to get ready their war ships and escort-vessels which were later found to be unsuitable to be put to sea. The Sultan of Miṣr (Egypt), Qānṣūh al-Ghawrī,[10] may Allah be pleased with him, had sent one of his Emirs, Amīr Ḥusayn, with thirteen ships and some troops. Amīr

Ḥusayn reached the Diu port in Gujarat. Then they sailed to Shiyūl[11] and with them were Malik Iyās,[12] the *nā'ib* at Diu, and his escort-vessels. They came across few Portuguese ships, and in the fight that ensued, Amīr Ḥusayn captured one big Portuguese ship.[13] Amīr Ḥusayn and his troops, then, returned to Diu with their ships. He stayed there for a few months during the rainy season. Subsequently, on the instruction of the Zamorin, about forty ships from his city and elsewhere arrived at Diu as reinforcement to Amīr Ḥusayn.

Learning about Amīr Ḥusayn and his men camping in Diu, the Portuguese set sail in twenty ships prepared for war and appeared suddenly before Diu. Responding to this unexpected Portuguese arrival, Amīr Ḥusayn, without preparation, put to sea his ships and those of Malik Iyās, together with the small ships that had come from Malabar. When the Portuguese met the combined forces, they fixed their attention upon the ships of Amīr Ḥusayn, and captured few of his ships while the remainder got separated. Thus by the decree of Allah and His indisputable command, the accursed Portuguese returned victorious to Kochi. Amīr Ḥusayn and a few of his soldiers could escape along with the troops of Malik Iyās, the Malabaris and their ships.[14] Amīr Ḥusayn returned to Egypt.

Qānṣūh al-Ghawrī, the Sultan of Miṣr, was indignant at the defeat and so he dispatched twenty-two ships fully equipped with all the paraphernalia of war, under the command of Amīr Salmān al-Rūmī along with Amīr Ḥusayn.

The forces of al-Ghawrī with their ships reached the well protected port of Jeddah and then proceeded to Camran port.[15] There, Amīr Ḥusayn started a war with the people of Yemen and plundered their country. Over this, Salmān al-Rūmī left him and sailed to the port of Aden, and then he returned to Jeddah. There in Jeddah, a fight broke out between Amīr Ḥusayn and Salmān al-Rūmī on account of Amīr Ḥusayn's fighting and plundering the Muslims. So Salmān had to leave Jeddah and return to his country. Amīr Ḥusayn was, before long, captured by Sultan al-Sharīf Barakāt[16] of Ḥijāz, and was killed by drowning in the sea. It was after these incidents, that news reached Jeddah that a war had erupted between Sultan Qānṣūh al-Ghawrī and Sultan Salīm Shāh al-Rūmī;[17] Qānṣūh al-Ghawrī had lost and was soon murdered, and Salīm Shāh al-Rūmī had captured his kingdom. Allah is the Master over His affairs.

On Thursday, 22nd of Ramaḍān, 915 AH (1510 AD), the Portuguese arrived at Calicut, attacking the city.[18] They set ablaze the congregational mosque there, which was built by the renowned Nākhudā Mithqāl.[19] Then they entered the Zamorin's palace claiming that they had captured it. The Zamorin was not present there at that time, he was elsewhere some distance away on matters related to war. The Nair soldiers in the palace fought the Portuguese intruders and routed them from the palace. They killed about five hundred of the soldiers on the Portuguese side. Many died drowning at sea and the rest fled to their ships in despair,[20] as Allah, exalted be He, willed.

Sometime before or after this incident, the Portuguese came to Ponnani and set fire to nearly fifty fishing boats they found unoccupied on the beach. Some seventy Muslims who fought them there were martyred.

Likewise, the Portuguese arrived at Aden[21] and had a fierce battle with the Muslims there. Allah helped the Muslims and abandoned the Portuguese and they had to flee for life, totally vanquished. This happened when Amīr Marjān was the ruler of Aden, may Allah be pleased with him.[22]

The Portuguese, after they made their positions secure in Kochi and Kannur, entered into a treaty with the King of Kollam and built a fort there.[23] Kochi and Kollam, those days, had been the centres that attracted most of the trade in pepper, more than any other places.

Then they fought the people of Goa[24] and captured Goa and occupied it.[25] The Goa port had been in the hands of Adil Shah, the grandfather of Ali Adil Shah the Great. The Portuguese made Goa their capital in India and established their rule there. But, before long, Adil Shah fought against the Portuguese and recaptured Goa and routed them from there. Thus, it once again became part of Islamic territory (*Dār al-Islām*). Infuriated by this, the Portuguese came back with massive preparations. They fought the Muslims there, captured Goa again and made it part of their domain.[26] It is said that Emirs and principal men of Goa had a clandestine understanding with the Portuguese; hence it was easy for them to recapture Goa.[a] Then the Portuguese built several forts and huge buildings and towers there. If Allah wills anything, He brings it to pass. Thus their power began to grow day by day.

---

a. From the available facts of history we do not know if the Emirs helped the Portuguese.

CHAPTER TWO

Certain Shameful Deeds of the Portuguese

At first, a condition prevailed in Malabar that allowed the Muslims there to lead a prosperous and comfortable life on account of the benevolence of their rulers, their time-honoured customs and their kindness. But, they belittled Allah's blessings, and transgressed and became heedless. So Allah set on them the Portuguese Christians and He, may He be exalted, abandoned them. They oppressed the Muslims, corrupted them and committed all kinds of ugly and infamous deeds against them, too bad to be described.[1]

The Portuguese scoffed at the Muslims and held them up to scorn. They harassed them for no reason; insulted them; humiliated them; forced them to carry them on their back to cross filthy, muddy tracts as they toured around the countryside; spit at them and on their faces; obstructed their journeys especially ḥajj journeys; plundered their wealth; seized their vehicles; set fire to their houses and mosques; trampled under feet and burned the Holy Qur'an and other religious books; reviled publicly the Prophet (s); defiled and polluted the places of worship; made them speak ill of and against the religion of Islam; forced them to bow before the cross and gave money to those who did so; paraded the Christian women fully adorned with rich ornaments and attired in fine clothes in front of the Muslim women to tempt the Muslim women; killed the ḥajj pilgrims and persecuted them with all kinds of cruelties; captured them and kept them bound in heavy chains on their feet or kept them handcuffed dragging them around in the streets and markets to sell them as slaves; and whenever anybody ventured to liberate them out of sympathy, flogged them mercilessly to exact bigger prices; captured them and kept them confined in filthy and stinky, overcrowded dark rooms in dangerous conditions; beat them with sandals and branded them with burning sticks for using water to clean themselves after execration, etc.; captured Muslims and sold some, enslaved some; forced them to do all kinds of hard labour without any compensation. These were among the things they usually did to the Muslims.

The Portuguese, after great preparations, sailed into the ports of Gujarat, Konkan[2] and Malabar, and the coast of Arabia, lay in wait for the ships of Muslims and seized them. Thereby they amassed abundant wealth and acquired a large number of Muslim prisoners. How many Muslim women of noble birth they took as captives, and violated their honour to bring into the world Christian children who would be enemies of the Faith of Allah, and agents to cause affliction to the Muslims! Many a scholars, members of the Holy Prophet's family, and other great personages were captured, held hostages, persecuted, and in the end killed brutally. Many Muslim men and women were forcefully converted to Christianity. How many such atrocities and cruelties! The tongues get weary of describing them and hate to put them in words. May Allah, the Almighty, chastise them for their crimes.

The ardent desire of the Portuguese at all times had been to make the Muslims renounce the faith of Islam and convert them to Christianity. May Allah protect us from such a fate! But the Portuguese had to maintain peaceful relations with the Muslims, out of necessity, for they had to live among the Muslims who formed the main body of populations in all the seaports of Malabar. So the newly arriving Portuguese men during certain seasons in the year, noticing the Muslims and their deportment in Kochi, said to their countrymen: "Until today the Muslims have not changed in their appearance." They blamed their predecessors for not doing enough to make the Muslims change their religion. "Fain would they extinguish Allah's light with their mouths, but Allah will not allow but that His Light should be perfected, even though the unbelievers may detest (it)." (Qur'an, 9:32)

Finally, they even appealed to the king of Kochi to expel the Muslims *en masse* from there. They tried to influence the king by telling him that his revenue from the Muslims is very meagre and that if he drives them all out from his territory, they would give him that revenue several times multiplied. The Kochi king's reply was that Muslims could not be expelled from his country as they were his subjects from time immemorial and besides, they were a great deal instrumental in the development and prosperity of the country. The Portuguese showed enmity only towards the Muslims and their Faith and not to Nairs or other unbelievers of Malabar.

The Zamorin-Portuguese Treaty and the Construction of the Portuguese Fort in Calicut

As the war prolonged, the weakness of the Muslims increased.[1] And the Zamorin who had spent big sum in these wars died and his younger brother succeeded him. This new king was of the view that peace with the Portuguese was the best course, for it would bring to his Muslim subjects prosperity in their trade like the prosperity enjoyed by those in Kannur and Kochi, and would remove their weakness and rescue them from their penury. And accordingly, he entered into a treaty with Portuguese by which he permitted the Portuguese to build a fort in Calicut on condition that they allow his Muslim subjects to undertake trade voyages to the Arabian port of Jeddah and Aden in four ships every year.[2]

Then the accursed Portuguese began to build a solid fort while the subjects of Zamorin set out to the Arabian ports in four ships laden with pepper and dried ginger. Like others, they too began to make trade trips as before to Gujarat and other destinations carrying passes from the Portuguese. This was in the year 920 or 921 AH (AD 1514-15).

By the time the first four ships to the Arabian ports returned to Calicut, the Portuguese had completed the construction of their fort in Calicut.[3] Then they forbade the Muslims from making further trips to the Arabian ports with pepper and ginger in their ships. Thus, they wanted to monopolise the trade in pepper and dried ginger. Whenever they saw even a small quantity of these two spices in any ship, they seized the ship, its contents and its crew. The Portuguese thus became the source of great affliction and distress to the Muslims and other subjects.

The Zamorin, who paid due regard to the peace, endured their evil doings with patience, because he was apprehensive of their wickedness. Nevertheless, he secretly sent letters to the Muslim Sultans urging them to make preparations for war with the Portuguese, but it was no avail. It was what Allah willed.

The Portuguese, may Allah curse them, were clever and deceitful. They know very well the course which is best for their business. They will be quite cordial and polite towards their enemies when necessary, but once they have achieved their aims, they treated them abominably. Among themselves, they are quite united in sentiment and conduct.[4] They do not disobey their elders even though they are far away from their rulers. It was rarely that disagreement in opinion happened among them, and nothing is so far heard about anybody among them murdering any of them for grabbing power. These were the reasons why the rulers of Malabar and others submitted to the Portuguese in spite of their being small in number. On the other hand, the Muslim soldiers and their Emirs quarrelled among themselves, and were striving to depose one another from power even by killing.[a]

---

a. This is a reference to the frequent quarrels between the Sultans of Bijapur, Ahmadnagar, Golkonda, Birar and Bidar, not to speak of their wars with the kings of Vijayanagar.

When the Portuguese had established themselves firmly in Calicut and stabilised their position, they invited the Zamorin to their residence within the fort on the pretext of giving him some precious gifts which were said to have been received by them from their king in Portugal. But their real design was to take him prisoner. The Zamorin, on reaching there, got a hint of it from the gesticulation of a Portuguese man. So he left the place quickly pretending to attend to a call of nature. Thus, by the grace of Allah, he could escape without falling into the trap laid for him by the treacherous Portuguese. The man who gave the hint to the Zamorin and whoever else involved in it were punished by being transferred from Calicut to Kannur.[5]

In the month of Muḥarram, 923 AH (1517 AD), the Portuguese set out from Goa with massive preparations for war, with a fleet of about twenty eight ships, having designs upon the well fortified port of Jeddah. When they reached the port, the Muslims there were terribly perturbed and in great fear. Salmān al-Rūmī, who had earlier been sent by Qānṣūh al-Ghawrī to help the Malabar Muslims against the Portuguese, was then present there with his warships and about two hundred soldiers. They opened fire at the Portuguese from the shore inflicting considerable damage to some of their ships. The Portuguese hoisted all sail, steered out of range of the cannon fire and fled in fear. But Salmān al-Rūmī sent thirty soldiers in two boats chasing them. They captured a Portuguese ship at Camran and returned to Jeddah with twelve Christians who were on board the ship. The Portuguese remained at Camran till the cessation of *mawsim al-Hind* (monsoon season) and returned to Goa, frustrated in their hopes. Such was the pleasure of Allah.

CHAPTER FOUR

The Rivalry between Zamorin and Portuguese, and the Capture of the Calicut Fort

Know now then: the Portuguese atrocities and excesses in Calicut increased day by day. But the Zamorin turned a blind eye to these atrocities. Their excesses continued until one day a fight broke out in Calicut between the Portuguese and some Muslims of the Pantalayani. The incident happened on 10 Muharram of 931 AH (1524 AD). Thus peace was broken and hostilities began. Also, about a year earlier in 930 AH, in an another incident, some people from Pantalayani, Chemmanad, Tirurangadi, Parappanangadi and a few other places, sailing in small boats, had captured about ten trade vessels belonging to the Portuguese.

Meanwhile a civil strife broke out in Kodungallur between the Muslims and the Jews of the locality. The Jews killed a Muslim that led to the riot. The Muslims sent messengers to their brethren in various towns of Malabar seeking their aid to retaliate upon the Jews. The inhabitants of Calicut with their relatives from Pantalayani, the people of Kakkad,[1] Tikkodi[2] with their relatives from Chaliyam, and people from Parappanangadi,[3] Tirurangadi,[4] Tanur,[5] Parawanna,[6] Ponnani,[7] and Weliancode[8] gathered in the Chaliyam Friday prayer mosque. There, they resolved to attack the Jews of Kodungallur. They also resolved to wage war against the Portuguese and not to make peace with them except with the permission of the Zamorin. This too occurred in the year 931AH (1524 AD).

Accordingly, they embarked in a fleet of about a hundred small vessels to Kodungallur and they killed several Jews there. The rest fled to the rural areas in the eastern parts of Kodungallur. The Muslims set ablaze the houses and the synagogues of the Jews. When they ventured to set fire the houses and churches belonging to the Christians, the Nair community protested and this caused a clash between the Muslims and the Nair community. And a few men of the Nair community were killed in the clash. For this reason, it became untenable for the Muslims of the locality to live there and they were forced to migrate to other places.

It was in the same year that people of Darmadam, Edakkad, Kannur,[9] Tiruwangad,[10] Ezhimala and Chemmanad,[11] joined forces to begin a war with the Portuguese. The Muslims in other towns also did likewise.

Also the same year, some of the chieftains of Kochi like Faqih Ahmad Marakkar,[12] his brother Kunhi Ali Marakkar, their uncle Muhammad Ali Marakkar and their followers felt the urge to fight the Portuguese and so they sailed from Kochi to Calicut. When the Portuguese became aware that most of the Muslims and the Zamorin were firmly opposed to them, with great preparation for war, they set sail from Kochi and landed at Ponnani on Saturday morning, 3 Jamādī al-Awwal, 931 AH. They burned down innumerable houses, business centres, warehouses and a few mosques on the shore. They felled and destroyed innumerable coconut palms on the shore. Many

Muslims suffered martyrdom. Then the Portuguese set sail on the second night of the arrival, and reached Pantalayani.[13] There, they seized some forty ships belonging to its inhabitants and others. Here again many Muslims fell martyrs.

When the discord broke out in Calicut between the Portuguese and some of the Pantalayani Muslims, the Zamorin resolved to fight against the Portuguese. But he was away at a place some distance away from Calicut, involved in another conflict with some of his enemies. So he sent his chief minister, al-Yadh,[a] with orders to fight against the Portuguese. Al-Yadh made massive preparations expending a huge amount of money. The Muslim warriors and the Nair troops of the Zamorin together besieged the Portuguese fort. Muslims from many parts of the country converged in Calicut with a zeal of waging holy war in the path of Allah. Then, the Zamorin himself arrived. By that time, the Portuguese had run out of provisions in the fort and they had no hope of getting fresh supplies of provisions from outside either. The Portuguese, in despair, burrowed the rear part of the fort unseen from outside and moved all their valuables to their ships and escaped. This took place in the year 932 AH (1525 AD).[14] By the time this campaign ended in victory, over two thousand people including Muslims, Nair warriors and the officers of the Zamorin had been killed. The Portuguese' enmity towards the Zamorin and the Muslims increased by the loss of their fort. And this state of affairs lasted for a very long time.

Since they had resolved to wage war on the Portuguese, the Muslims began to make trade trips by ships without a license

____

a. It appears the Zamorin had four *wazīrs*. They were Accan of Mangat (Mangat Achan), Elayadu of Tenanceri (Tenanceri Elayatu) near Malappuram, and two others. The *wazīr* mentioned in the text was probably Elayadu.

from the Portuguese, fully prepared for war. They carried dried ginger, pepper, etc. to Gujarat and few other places. Although some of those ships could escape from the Portuguese, most of them were captured or stranded on land because of this.[15] As a result, people of Darmadam and their allies volunteered to make peace with the Portuguese towards the close of the season, and started their trade trips with license from the Portuguese as before. But the Zamorin and his subjects continued their confrontation with the Portuguese for years. This weakened their power and exhausted their resources.

In the year 935 AH (1528 AD), during the early monsoon period, a Portuguese vessel shipwrecked at Tanur[16] in the beginning of the rainy season. The king of Tanur gave shelter to those who were on board. The Zamorin wrote to the Tanur king demanding to hand over to him the ship, her merchandise and the people on board. But the Zamorin's demand was refused. This prompted the Tanur king to conclude a pact with the Portuguese by which the people of Tanur were to resume their trade trips with license from the Portuguese, and the Portuguese were to build a fort on the northern side of the Ponnani River, which was under his territory. The main purpose behind the idea of building the fort here was to weaken the position of the Zamorin, harass the travellers and to cripple Ponnani.[17]

To build the fort, the Portuguese set out from Kochi in many ships and boats carrying bricks and quicklime, and anchored off Ponnani. It might have been perhaps Allah's help to the Zamorin and the Muslims, all those ships and boats were wrecked in a fierce storm and some of them were cast away on the southern side of Weliancode. Only a small boat escaped the ravages. Several people including the Portuguese, their workers and slaves drowned at sea. And of those who managed to escape to the shore, several were caught and killed. A great number of men who were prisoners in the hands of the Portuguese were set free by the Muslims. The Zamorin gained all the big cannons. Thus the clandestine plot of the Portuguese and their local allies here was thwarted.

In the year 937 or 938 AH (1530-31 AD) the subjects of the Zamorin and a few others from outside together made a trade trip in about thirty ships to various ports of Gujarat. The party included Ali Ibrahim Marakkar, his nephew Kutty Ibrahim Marakkar and their friends and a few other important people. Most of them got off at Jujar and Surat and a few others at Barooj.[18] Learning about this, the Portuguese set out in ships and boats for war with them. They also got off at the ports of Jujar and Surat. They seized the ships which were harboured there together with the merchandise. Those who got off at Barooj managed to escape.

Before this incident, many ships belonging to Bahadur Shah, the Gujarat Sultan and the people of Malabar, had, by misfortune, fallen into the hands of the Portuguese on various occasions.

The Second Zamorin-Portuguese Treaty, and the Construction of the Portuguese Fort at Chaliyam

One of the top Portuguese officials[a] set out from Kochi by land in the name of peace, concealing deceit and treachery, to present himself before the Zamorin. He was very intelligent and cunning. This man had good rapport with some Muslim notables during the time when the Portuguese were in a treaty relationship with the Zamorin before.[1]

Arriving at Ponnani, this Portuguese man went straight to the Tanur king. He stayed with him till he brought about peace between him and the Zamorin.

The Zamorin, who captured the Portuguese fort of Calicut, was a weak and feeble-minded monarch, and he was grossly addicted to drinking, while his brother Nanbiyadhar, who was to succeed him after his death, was a strong, shrewd, brave man. He was noted for his recalcitrant attitude towards their ancient customs prevalent among them.

The peace agreement the Zamorin made with the Tanur king brought great suffering to the ruler of Tanur, the Zamorin himself and his officials and his successors, since it has allowed

---

a. The name of this high official is not known.

the Portuguese to build the fort at Chaliyam which was on the sea route of the Zamorin and his troops. It is also on the route of travellers from many countries. The trade trips from Calicut to their destinations in Arabia through Chaliyam, situated only at a distance of about eight miles from Calicut, also suffered. However, after discussing matters with the king of Chaliyam, the Zamorin at last permitted the Portuguese to build a fort there. And the Portuguese, very soon, arrived at Chaliyam in a huge ship, loaded with materials needed for the construction of the fort. They entered Chaliyam River towards the end of the month of Rabī' al-Ākhir in the year 938 AH (1531 AD) and constructed a strong fort, at the same time demolishing the ancient Masjid al-Jāmi' (congregation mosque)[2] that had been built in the early stage of the advent of Islam to Malabar—of which mention has already been made—along with two other mosques. They used the blocks and other materials of the demolished mosques for building the fort and a church inside the fort.

In the course of the construction of the fort, at first a Portuguese man came and burrowed out one block of the wall of the congregation mosque, mentioned above, and took it away. The Muslims complained to the leader of the Portuguese about this. Immediately the officer came with a group of workers and patched up the burrowed out part using blocks and cement. That act gladdened the Muslims of the locality and they returned home cheerfully and with gratitude.

The second day of the incident, the Portuguese came in a big group and pulled down the entire mosque. They did not spare a single brick. The Muslims again approached the leader of the Portuguese and complained, but he told them that the mosque and its site had been sold to them by their king.[3] The Muslims returned grief stricken. After that they used to assemble in a small mosque which was situated far. The Portuguese did not stop there. Those wicked devils broke open the graves and tombs of the Muslims on the site and used their bricks and blocks for the construction of the fort.

Before the completion of the construction of the fort, the Zamorin who allowed its construction died, and his younger brother, Nanbiyadhar, assumed power as the new Zamorin. He annulled the pact and declared war on the Chaliyam king. He laid waste the territory of Chaliyam king and the king eventually surrendered to the Zamorin and had a pact with him according to ancient customs and conventions prevailing on such matters at that time.[4]

The same year, Amīr Muṣṭafā al-Rūmī[5] arrived at Diu port in Gujarat from Mocha (Muqwa)[6] with cannon and vast treasure. Mālik Tughan, son of Malik Iyās, was the governor of Diu on behalf of Sultan Bahadur Shah at that time. Learning about the arrival of Muṣṭafā al-Rūmī, the Portuguese rushed to the place to bring the Diu port under their control. Amīr Muṣṭafā met them with the cannons. By the will of Allah, the Portuguese were routed and they fled the place, shamefully defeated and humiliated.

CHAPTER SIX

The Third Zamorin–Portuguese Treaty

In the year 940 AH (1533 AD) the Zamorin made peace with the Portuguese on certain conditions: One of the conditions was that the Zamorin's subjects will send from Calicut at least four ships annually with merchandises to the Arabian shores. Accordingly, a fleet of four ships fully laden with merchandises set out to Arabia the same year. The Zamorin's subjects also started to go on trade trips to other countries as well with the license from the Portuguese.

Then, the Zamorin declared war on the Tanur king and fought him and subjugated him until peace was restored between them by which the Tanur king was made to cede to Zamorin several territories adjacent to Ponnani and a little isle near Chaliyam. The mediator for the pact was the Portuguese gentleman who had come from Kochi for the construction of their fort at Chaliyam.[1]

On the heels of the treaty between the Zamorin and the Portuguese, Khawājah Ḥusayn Zanjaqdār al-Rūmī and Faqih Ahmad Marakkar's brother Kunhi Marakkar arrived by ship at Calicut shore on 16 Rabī' al-Awwal, 941 AH (1534 AD). They had been sent to the Zamorin with many presents and gifts by Sultan Bahadur Shah. The Sultan's request was that the Zamorin send Malabar Muslims to Gujarat to fight the Portuguese at sea. But this was of no avail.[2]

Conclusion of Peace between Sultan Bahadur Shah and the Portuguese; and the Surrender of Some of his Ports to the Portuguese

As soon as Humayun[a] son of Sultan Babar,[1] (May Allah fill their graves with light!) assumed power in Delhi towards the end of the year 941 AH (1535 AD), he turned his attention to Gujarat. He attacked and destroyed some of the cities in Gujarat. The Gujarat ruler Sultan Bahadur Shah was routed. Filled with terror and afraid of Humayun, Bahadur Shah sent messengers to the Portuguese for help. The Portuguese were quick to respond and a treaty was concluded between them, the Sultan ceding few of his ports like Vasai, Mahim,[2] etc. to the Portuguese. The Portuguese took possession of these ports and extended their domain by annexing the surrounding region.

The Portuguese gained great advantages by this treaty and their power and influence increased. The Sultan also surrendered

---

a. Humayun Badshah was the Mughal Emperor between 1530 and 1540 and 1555 and 1556 AD. During the years 1540 and 1555 AD, he was a wanderer, as he was deprived of his empire by Sher Shah.
Babar Badshah (Zahiruddin Muhammad) was the founder of the Mughal empire in India. He ruled at Delhi between 1526 and 1530 AD.

to the Portuguese the control over the port of Diu and charged them with its government. For this the Portuguese were to get half of the revenue collected there. Thus the Portuguese ruled Diu and fortified it.

In the past, the Portuguese were longing to get possession of the island Diu and had made several attempts to capture it during the reign of Malik Iyās and later during the reign of his sons. But they were never able to subdue it and they always returned disappointed in their hopes by Allah's will. This time their wish and Allah's decree coincided, and so it was made easy for them. Allah, glory be to Him and exalted be He, had also decreed that Sultan Bahadur Shah should die by their hands.[3] They killed him and threw his body into the sea. Verily we are from Allah and to Him we return! It happened on 3 Ramaḍān, 943 AH (1537 AD). After the martyrdom of the Sultan, Diu as a whole came under the Portuguese control and they settled there. Such was the decree of Allah, the All-Wise and the All-Powerful. No one shall repel the judgement of Allah or dispute His will.

In the year 944 AH (1537 AD), the Portuguese fell upon to Paravanna and killed Kutty Ibrahim Marakkar, son of Umar Ali Ibrahim Marakkar [4] and those of his friends with him. They also set the city ablaze and then they returned. This happened notwithstanding the fact the treaty with the Tanur king was still in force and the people of Tanur and Parawanna were making trade trips with license from them. The reason for this act of violence was that Kutty Ibrahim reportedly sent a ship laden with pepper and dried ginger to Jeddah port without license from the Portuguese. The one thing the Portuguese detested most was trade trips by others in pepper and dried ginger to other places, especially to Jeddah.

Then the Zamorin set out to Kodungallur to fight the Portuguese and the ruler of Kochi. The war lasted many days, and Allah infused into Zamorin's mind a dread of them and consequently he returned from there without achieving anything. Then the Portuguese built a fort at Kodungallur.[a] It was a strong barrier for Zamorin to take on.

It was after this incident that Ali Ibrahim Marakkar and Faqih Ahmad Marakkar and his brother Kunhi Marakkar (may Allah's blessings be upon them) left for Kayal Pattanam[5] in a fleet of forty two vessels. When they reached Puttalam,[6] they harboured the ships and stayed there for days and became vain and idle. The Portuguese arrived there in few ships and fought and, as destined by Allah, captured all their ships. Many in the party of Marakkar fell martyrs in the confrontation. This happened in the month of Sha'ban in the year 944 AH (1538 AD). Those who survived returned to Malabar. Near Nallambilly[7] on the way, Ali Ibrahim Marakkar died. May Allah shower on him His generous mercy and blessings!

The Portuguese had captured a few ships belonging to the people of Kakkad near Kannur the same year. May Allah ruin those devilish transgressors!

---

a. The fort was constructed in 1537 AD.

CHAPTER EIGHT

Sulaymān Bāshā's Visit to Diu and the Neighbouring Places

It was also in 944 AH (1538 AD) that Sulaymān Bāshā,[1] the *wazīr* of Turkish Sultan Sulaymān Shāh,[2] about whom mention was already made, arrived at Aden port fully prepared for war, with a fleet of hundred warships, several cargo boats, and other paraphernalia of war. He killed Shaykh 'Āmir bin Dāwūd, the Sultan of the place, and a few other important people there and captured the port.[3] Then he marched against Gujarat and fell upon Diu. He destroyed the major portion of fort walls with the huge cannons he brought with him. In the course of the fight, Allah instilled fear of Portuguese in the mind of Sulaymān Bāshā and he returned to Egypt [4] and from there, he left for Rome. When the Portuguese arrived at Diu, they repaired and rebuilt the forts and made them more secure.

One year after Ali Ibrahim Marakkar's death, Faqih Ahmad Marakkar and his brother Kunhi Marakkar set out to Ceylon in a fleet of eleven ships. Learning about this, the Portuguese chased them and fought and captured their ships. Many among them were martyred and those who survived went ahead to meet the king of Ceylon. Faqih Ahmad Marakkar and Kunhi Marakkar were among them. However, the king of Ceylon murdered them treacherously.[5] Verily we are for Allah and to Allah we return.

CHAPTER NINE

The Fourth Zamorin-Portuguese Treaty

In Sha'bān, 946 AH (1540 AD), the Portuguese came to the Zamorin seeking peace. He was then in Ponnani, and peace was concluded in the presence of Tanur king and the Kodungallur King. Following this, the Zamorin's subjects began to undertake trade trips carrying with them passes from the Portuguese.[1]

Then, on 8 Muḥarram, 952 AH (1545 AD), the Portuguese killed a prominent leader of Kannur, Abu Bakar Ali. Also killed with him was his brother in law, Kunhi Sooppy. Abu Bakar Ali was the uncle of Arakkal Ali Adhraja[2] and Kunhi Sooppy, his father, may Allah's blessings be upon them. This caused a long-lasting hostility between the Portuguese and the people of Kannur. Eventually peace was established.[3]

CHAPTER TEN

Hostility between the Zamorin and the Portuguese

A treaty was signed on 1 Muḥarram, 957 AH (1550 AD) between the Zamorin and one of the rulers of Malabar, who was the important ally of the ruler of Kochi and whose territory was adjoining to Kochi on the southern side.[1] The Portuguese calls him 'pepper king'[a] because large quantities of pepper were exported from his towns. He became one of the allies of the Zamorin and gave him his kingdom. In return, the Zamorin will recognise his brother as the fourth in line of succession to the Zamorin. The Zamorin accordingly made his brother the fourth in the succession in accordance with the ancient custom prevalent in Malabar.

When the 'pepper king' returned to his town, the ruler of Kochi and the Portuguese arrived there to wage war against him and in the battle followed, the pepper king was burnt to death. This happened in Jamādī al-Awwal, 957 AH (1550 AD).

When news of the pepper king's death reached the Zamorin, he set out immediately from Calicut to fight the Portuguese and their ally. He reached the town of the pepper king and fought the

a. Evidently the author refers to the Raja of Vatakkenkur (also called Pimienta) who was a friend of the Zamorin. His territory lay to the south-east of Cochin. (See K. P. Padmanabha Menon, *History of Kerala*, Vol. I pp. 502-03).

Portuguese and the Kochi king. He had to expend huge amount of his wealth for this, but returned to Calicut, without gaining anything neither for himself or his ally.

On 8 Jamādī al-Ākhir, the same year, large body of the troops of the pepper king crossed the river and entered Kochi. They set ablaze every house they passed by. The devastation they caused to Kochi was immense. They did so because their king was killed in the fight against the ruler of Kochi and the Portuguese. May Allah chastise them with severe chastisement. This caused the conflict between the Zamorin and the Portuguese. The Portuguese set out from Goa with massive preparations for war and landed at Tikkodi. They burnt down the houses, the trade centres and the big *jum'ah* mosque there. This happened on Saturday, 14 Shawwāl, 957 AH (1550 AD). They arrived at Pantalayani the second day of this incident and burnt down the houses and shops there and also the big *jum'ah* mosque built in the early stage of the spread of Islam. The following Thursday, they landed at Ponnani at daybreak and set ablaze several houses, warehouses and four mosques including the big *jum'ah* mosque there. In all these three towns, a large number of Muslims were martyred.[2]

Towards the end of Jamādī al-Ākhir, 960 AH (1553 AD) a report spread widely in Malabar to the effect that 'Alī al-Rūmī, one of the military leaders of the Muslims, was martyred in the course of his fight with the Portuguese near Keelakkara[3] and that all his ships were captured. May Allah destroy the Portuguese as He destroyed the 'Ād and the Thamūd.[4] *Verily we are for Allah and to Allah we return!* Such is the decree of Allah, the All-Powerful and the All-Knowing. It was just before this incident that 'Alī al-Rūmī had captured a few of the Portuguese ships and landed at Punnakkayal near Kayal Pattanam where the Portuguese were taking up residence. He attacked and put the Portuguese to rout and devastated the place.

In Rajab, 960 AH (1553 AD), a Turk by the name of Yūsuf, arrived at Ponnani from the Maldives, notwithstanding it was not the season for trade trips.[5] He came with a number of very huge cannons captured from the Portuguese who were living on the island.[6]

Chapter Eleven

The Fifth Zamorin–Portuguese Treaty

When the Portuguese continued with their activities in the same way, the weakness and poverty of Muslims increased. So the Zamorin concluded a treaty with the Portuguese and the Zamorin's subjects began to undertake trade trips, like others, with license from the Portuguese. This treaty happened in early Muḥarram, 963 AH (1555 AD).

About two years or more after this treaty, the Muslims of Kannur, Darmadam, and their neighbourhoods had serious disputes with the Portuguese.[1] These lasted about two years. Then peace was restored and the people of these localities resumed their trade trips with the license from the Portuguese, as they used to do before.

During the period of the struggle against the Portuguese, Ali Adhraja, who was a great leader, energetic and zealous, spent a large amount of money in that war. But the ruler Kolattiri and his subjects in other towns did not lend support to Adhraja. It was during that period the accursed Portuguese started out in angry mood to despoil Adhraja of his islands[2] in Malabar.[a] The Portuguese went in their corvettes and attacked the island of Amini where they killed a large number of inhabitants, captured

---

a. This is a reference to the group of islands known as the Laccadives. One of the islands in the group was Amini, which even now goes by the same name.

more than four hundred men and women, plundered almost everything of value, and burned many houses and mosques. Before they descended upon Amini, they went to Shaytalkam (Chetlatt) where they slew some of the people and captured some.

The inhabitants of all these islands were ignorant of the use of weapons, and there was none capable to fight. Notwithstanding this, a large number of the people fought against the enemy and fell as martyrs. Of them their *qāḍī* (religious leader and judge) and a pious woman were worthy of note. The *qāḍī* was an elderly person, virtuous and pious. Though the inhabitant of that island possessed no arms, they were prepared to give testimony to their faith in their religion and die as martyrs. They flung earth and stones at the Portuguese and inflicted blows on them severely with sticks till they were killed. May Allah wrap them with His Infinite Mercy.

The islands off Malabar Coast are many in number but the big ones which are like cities are five: Amini, Kardib, Andur, Kalfini and Malki. Of the small islands, the thickly populated ones are Akti, Kanjamanjala, Kaltan and Shaytlakam.[3]

When Allah, glory be to Him and exalted be He, wished to put His servants to test, He granted respite to the Portuguese. He enabled them to establish their power in a large number of ports like the seaports of Malabar, Gujarat, Konkan and other places. They had their sway over these places by opening trade factories in most of these towns. They built fortresses in Hurmuz (Ormuz, Persian Gulf), Masqat (Maskat), Dewmahall (Maldives), Shamtara (Sumatra), Malaqa (Malacca), Maluku (Moluccas), Mylapur, Nakfatan and in other seaports of Sholamandal (Coromandel), and also in many ports of Silan (Ceylon). Further they had reached as far as China. Their trade was flourishing in these ports and elsewhere, while the Muslim merchants in these places were humbled and made to submit to the Portuguese as servants.

The Muslim merchants were not permitted to trade in all commodities except in goods in which the Portuguese had little interest. The commodities in which the Portuguese had interest yielded large profits. They assumed exclusive rights to trade in such commodities, and it was not possible for others to encroach on their rights. They started their monopoly with pepper and ginger but gradually added to the list cinnamon, clove, spice and such other articles, which yielded large profits. The Muslims were forbidden to trade in all these articles and or to undertake sea-voyages for trade purposes to the Arabian coast, Malacca, Ashi (probably Aceh, North Sumatra), Danasri[4] and other places. Thus there remained nothing for the Muslims of Malabar, but the petty trade in areca nut, cocoanut, clothes and such other things. Their sea-traffic also was confined to Gujarat, Konkan, Sholamandal and round about Qail.

The Portuguese built forts in Honnawaram,[5] Basarur and Mangalore to prevent the Muslims from bringing rice from these places to Goa and Malabar, and likewise to the ports of Arabia. The Portuguese, may God destroy them, became importers of merchandise from different part of the world, stored them in various parts of the districts and continued to augment it. The rulers in different seaports submitted themselves to them to such an extent that the authority of the Portuguese in these places became supreme. Before long, it became impossible for the Muslims to travel at sea anywhere in the world except under their protection and with their papers. Thus there was much trade for the Portuguese and they owned many ships. On the other hand there was little traffic on the sea for the Muslims and their trade had to be carried on through the ships of the Portuguese.

No one ventured to capture the forts built by the Portuguese. Only the brave Sultan Ali al-Ashi,[6] may Allah fill his grave with light. The Sultan captured Sumatra and turned it into an Islamic state, may Allah reward him for this service to the Muslims; the Zamorin the ruler of Calicut, captured the Portuguese forts in Calicut and Chaliyam; and the Ceylon king captured all the forts the Portuguese had built in his country, but these forts were not built as invincible as the rest of their forts.

In the early stage, the Portuguese honoured and gave security to the licenses they had issued. And they had not interrupted or harmed any trader with the license except for some special reason. By 960 AH (1558 AD), they issued license to whosoever sought it at the beginning of the journey but stopped the ships in the open sea, captured them, looted their merchandises and killed the travellers brutally regardless of whether they were Muslims or non-Muslims. They killed the travellers in wicked manner, such as hacking, throwing overboard into sea with their limbs fully bound, or tying a number of them together in nets and cast them into the seas.[7]

In 970 AH (1562 AD) or shortly before, they captured a group of Ethiopian Muslims in Goa. They forced them to convert to Christianity. They tortured them until they converted outwardly. When they escaped from their hold and left Goa, all of them returned to Islam glorifying Allah. One Abyssinian woman whom the Portuguese compelled to accept Christianity, refused, and she was put to death. May Allah shower on her His mercy and blessings!

Cause of the Zamorin and Portuguese Rivalry, and the Beginning of the Portuguese Setback

The Muslim strength decreased and their maritime trade all over came to a stop because of the heavy handed acts of the Portuguese. Then the Muslims of Walapattanam, Tikkodi, Pantalayani and few other places organized themselves and, without obtaining the Portuguese license, set out at sea in cargo boats, with weapons and ammunition ready for war. Soon they encountered the Portuguese and in the battle followed they captured several Portuguese ships and boats. This stirred the subjects of the Zamorin in Calicut, Ponnani, Puttanangadi, and Kakkad, and they too captured many of the Portuguese ships and boats and took many Portuguese captives. Through these enterprises, a lot of Portuguese wealth came into Muslim hands. They also captured a great number of ships that belonged to the unbelievers of Gujarat, Konkan and other places. In consequence of these activities, the Portuguese could not, ever since, undertake trips at sea without great precaution and the escorts of fully equipped warships.

This situation eventually led to the economic setback of the Portuguese. This in turn reduced for the Muslims the opportunity to capture their wealth. Thus there prevailed a situation in which Muslims started looting one another. The reasons often ascribed to this state of affairs are that most of the Muslim owners of corvettes were not rich and their ships were jointly owned by several people. Thus they were compelled to seek the means to recover, before they returned to shore, as much money as they had spent when they set out to sea. When they find what they have captured from the Portuguese was insufficient, they did not hesitate to grab from whomsoever they can, Muslim or non-Muslim. Although they had taken an oath when they set out for the trip that they would not stretch their hands to the wealth of the Muslims, they did not, in practice, return whatever had come to their hands even if they came to know that it belonged to the Muslims. They do not have a leader with power to pass judgement over them! Those who rule over the country were interested only in getting their share of the looted wealth. Mere advice and good counsel will benefit only those who are self conscious and pious, and such men are few among them.

About the middle of Ramaḍān, 974 AH (1566 AD), a group of people of Ponnani, Pantalayani and other places set out from Ponnani in about twelve ships. They captured a huge cargo boat belonging to the Portuguese which was bringing rice and sugar from Bengal to Ponnani.

On Saturday, 8 Jamādī al-Ākhir, 976 AH (1568 AD), another group of people from Ponnani, Pantalayani and some other places set out from Ponnani in seventeen ships. Kutty Pocker[1] was in the group. They came face to face with a huge Portuguese cargo ship near Chaliyam. That cargo boat was coming from Kochi. On board were about a thousand people, soldiers, many new converts to Christianity, and slaves, with a lot of wealth and equipments. A fierce battle took place between them. In the course of the struggle the cargo ship caught fire and burnt down completely. The Muslims managed to get a few cannons from it. And they could capture about a hundred Portuguese soldiers, a few dignitaries, several slaves and a few servants. The rest perished either in fire or drowning. Praise be to Allah.

After a few days of the incident, the same Muslim group set out to Kayal Pattanam. On their way, they captured twenty-two ships belonging to the Portuguese. Those ships, coming with rice from Kayal Pattanam, Coromandel and other places, had on board a number of new converts to Christianity and three little elephants. The Muslims captured the new Christian converts, and brought the little elephants ashore near the Ponnani River.

Towards the end of Jamādī al-Ākhir, 978 AH (1570 AD), Kutty Pocker entered the Mangalore River with six ships at night. He went ashore and set fire almost all the Portuguese forts, then captured one small Portuguese ship and returned safe, with all his ships intact. On his way, he met with about fourteen Portuguese ships near Kannur. He died a martyr in the confrontation with them. His body could not be recovered. Of the ships, only two could manage to escape. May Allah bless Kutty Pocker! He was indeed a sincere fighter who bravely fought the Portuguese.

A leading figure of Kannanur, Arakkal Ali Adhraja, may he blessed by God, perceiving the poverty, miseries and collapse of trade the Muslims were suffering from because of the accursed Portuguese, wrote to the great generous Sultan of Bijapur, Ali Adil Shah, seeking his help to wage *jihād* in the way of God for the purpose of rescuing these Muslims who were becoming weaker on account of the cruelty of Portuguese. He also sent several gifts to Adil Shah along with the letter.

Allah infused in the Sultan's mind to make preparations for war towards the Goa port which was the headquarters of the Portuguese in India. Goa once belonged to Sultan Adil Shah, Ali Adil Shah's grandfather. After destroying Vijayanagar and killing its king, Adil Shah and Nizam Shah,[2] the ruler of Ahmad Nagar, may Allah be pleased with both, came to an agreement to conquer Goa port and Chaul.

Soon after he received the letter from Adhraja, Sultan Ali Adil Shah started in person with his ministers, arrived at the Goa port and commenced fighting against the Portuguese. He blocked the food and provisions reaching the Portuguese. Then Ali Adil Shah wrote a letter to the Zamorin informing him that he had started hostilities against the Portuguese in Goa. He wrote to the Zamorin that he and his people should assist him in this war and cut off supplies to the Portuguese. Already Zamorin and his subjects were, for years, in a state of open hostility against the Portuguese. The letter was delivered to him through a messenger[3] at Chaliyam where he was engaged in a war with the Portuguese at that time.

In the meanwhile, Nizam Shah and his ministers arrived at Chaul with their forces and began hostilities with the Portuguese there. They destroyed the Portuguese forts there using big cannons. They were winning the war and they were on the verge of conquering the Chaul port. At that particular stage a suspicion occurred in Nizam Shah about Adil Shah. Also he felt frightened about the Portuguese power and might! Abruptly he stopped the war and made a treaty with the Portuguese.

As for Sultan Adil Shah, he might be exonerated from blame for the failure in his own undertaking. Goa was far away from his encampment, and also the river lay between him and the city. Further the fortress at Goa was strong and inaccessible with extensive fortifications and it was not possible for any one to subjugate it except with the help of the Almighty Allah. Besides, some of his ministers had already established clandestine rapport with the Portuguese and planning to imprison Adil Shah and hand over the kingship to one of his relatives in Goa who was on good terms with the Portuguese. Confronted with all these, in his helplessness, Adil Shah had sneaked out from his military headquarters and left the place. Arriving back at his palace, Adil Shah searched out those of his ministers who were spying for the Portuguese, removed them from offices and punished them by imprisonment. Then Adil Shah concluded peace with the Portuguese on account of certain important reasons. The Portuguese, meanwhile, built more invincible structures in Goa and fortified it strongly making it impossible for any outsider to have access to it. This is ordained by Allah, the All-Powerful and the All-Wise.

Nizam Shah, his ministers as well as the ministers of Adil Shah betrayed Adil Shah. They had been secretly delivering food and other provisions to them taking bribes. Let them receive from Allah the due reward for doing this help to the enemies of Islam.

CHAPTER THIRTEEN

The War that Ended in the Conquest of the Chaliyam Fort

The Zamorin stood firm with the resolution to lay siege to Chaliyam[a] fort on account of the transgression of the Portuguese and the earnest request of the Muslims, especially their entreaty that he should avail himself of the opportunity at the time of the Muslim expedition to Goa, because the Portuguese on that occasion will not be able to send ships and troops in support from Goa to Chaliyam.

The Zamorin sent to Chaliyam few of his ministers and with them were the people of Ponnani who were joined by people of Chaliyam. These were joined on their way by people from Parawanna, Tanur and Parappanangadi. All of them arrived at Chaliyam and camped there on Wednesday, 25 Ṣafar, 979 AH (1571 AD). Fighting between them and the Portuguese began by daybreak itself. The Muslims set fire to the houses and churches the Portuguese had built outside the fort and tore down the fort's outer wall which was built of mud. Only three persons from among the Muslims were martyred in this struggle. But on the Portuguese side, several people were killed. The Portuguese

---

a. The Zamorin besieged the fort of Shaliyat (Chaliyam) in 1571. The siege lasted for four months, and at the end of the period the Portuguese were completely defeated.

sought refuge inside the stonewalled main fort. The Muslims and the Nair forces besieged the fort. By then, several Muslims from various parts of the country joined them to take part in this holy struggle against the Portuguese. They dug deep ditches around the fort and remained outside on guard. With this, the chances of reaching food and other provisions into the fort secretly from outside became very remote.

The Zamorin spent a lot of his wealth for this war. After two months of the commencement of the war, the Zamorin personally arrived at Chaliyam. The Portuguese were still remaining inside the fort, completely besieged. When they had run out of food and other provisions, they began to eat the meat of animals such as dogs that nobody would like to eat. Since they didn't have anything to feed them with, they began to send out the slaves and those men and women they had converted to Christianity by force, in small numbers every day. And the Muslims let them go free, too. Although provisions arrived from Kochi and Kannur for the Portuguese, they couldn't reach them inside the fort, howsoever they tried. For this, they even had fights with the Muslims who were guarding outside the ditches. But that too didn't yield any result. Eventually, as the siege lasted for long, they sent an envoy to the Zamorin suing for peace. They informed the Zamorin that they shall give him a few huge cannons in the fort and compensate him for all the wealth that he had to spend for this war and a lot more. It was not acceptable to the Zamorin. But his ministers thought the terms quite acceptable.

The Portuguese were terribly distressed by food shortage. And, in their helplessness, they approached the Zamorin again. This time, what they informed him was that he may take whatever he likes including their fort and everything inside, only that they should be delivered alive to a place of safety with a handful of things that they can take with them. This the Zamorin accepted. Accordingly, in the midnight of Monday, 16 Jamādī al-Ākhir, 979 AH (1571 AD), they were allowed to march out of the fort, giving them a safe passage. They were sent away in despicable condition along with the ruler of Tanur who had been aiding and abetting them. The Tanur king was inwardly favourable to their cause but outwardly pretended to be a friend of the Zamorin. Thus he took responsibility for them, did whatever was found necessary for them, took them to Tanur and let them stay there until the Portuguese ships from Kochi came and took them away. For this help, the Tanur king had a big place and influence with the Portuguese. The Portuguese freed from the Chaliyam fort thus arrived at Kochi fully defeated and in deep humiliation.

Once the Portuguese abandoned the fort, the Zamorin took away the cannons and other valuables inside it and demolished the fort completely leaving no trace. The building blocks, bricks and timber from the demolished fort, he gave for rebuilding the mosque that had situated there before the construction of the fort. The remainder he transported to Calicut. The site of the fort and the surroundings were handed over to the Chaliyam king in accordance with the understanding at the commencement of the war.[1] The ships and the cargo boats the Portuguese had sent from Goa for the protection of the fort arrived at Chaliyam only after the Zamorin's capture of the fort. Their fate was to go back in despair and humiliation. The truth was that Allah's mercy favoured the Muslims.

CHAPTER FOURTEEN

The State of the Portuguese after the Loss of the Chaliyam Fort

The accursed Portuguese were in a fit of violent anger over the subjugation of their fort at Chaliyam. They were raging at the Zamorin and the Muslims, and were ever since on the lookout for an opportunity to avenge it. Their plan was to continuously torment the Muslims and the Zamorin and destroy his kingdom; and it was to be achieved by building a fort either in Ponnani or in Chaliyam. But Allah did not make it easy for them to accomplish their purpose until the close of the year 987 AH (1580 AD).

On 22 Shawwāl, 980 AH (1573 AD), some Portuguese descended at Chaliyam without any warning or signal, setting fire to some houses and shops. Then they left the place. The following year, they suddenly attacked Parappanangadi, and in the fight ensued, four Muslims were martyred while many died on the side of the enemy. Yet, they were not inclined to make peace with the Zamorin after his capture of Chaliyam port and cherished hatred of him and the Muslims, and were lying in wait for an opportunity to avenge their defeat.

In 985 AH (1577 AD), the Portuguese captured more than fifty ships, big and small, belonging to the Muslims bound for Talaimannar[1] to load rice. Many Muslims were martyred in the confrontations and nearly three thousand people were taken prisoners, among them there were a few from Halatia;[2] this was a big blow to the Muslims. This defeat badly affected all their travels including trade trips. This is a decree from Allah, the All-Mighty and All-Knowing! No one understands the wisdom and goodness behind this except He. A glorious reward waits for those who take part in *jihād,* who suffer martyrdom and endure with patience all misfortunes. We beseech Allah, may He be glorified, that the Muslims may be shown an opening soon and they be given great capacity for forbearance, noble and sublime! Indeed Allah says: "After a difficulty Allah will soon grant relief" (Qur'an, 65:7). And again He says, "Verily, with every difficulty there is relief" (94:5-6).[3]

The accursed Portuguese also captured a few Gujarati ships that were on their way back after their trips from Surat to Jeddah in the early days of the trade season of 985 AH. Some of these ships belonged to Sultan Jalaluddin Akbar Badshah,[4] and contained precious commodities. This wickedness on the part of the Portuguese brought about enmity between them and the Sultan. The Portuguese, however, did not care to return his ships as they were full of precious cargo. We hope Allah, glory be to Him, would guide Akbar Badshah to take the right decision and Allah will help him with great help to wage war against the Portuguese and drive them out of all the Gujarati ports, like Diu, Vasai, etc., which they were occupying.

Afterwards some ships belonging to the Muslims sailed into the river where the Adilabad port[5] was situated. The Portuguese chased them; when they could not catch up with them, they set fire to the whole harbour intent on burning every vessel that lay there, although some of the ships belonged to the people of Kannur, Darmadam, etc., who were on trade trips with the license from the Portuguese.

The Portuguese afterwards burned the Karapatanam Port, too. As a consequence of this, the governor of Dabul[6] captured hundred and fifty Portuguese soldiers including their chief officers and brave soldiers by some ruse. Many of them he killed and a few he sent to Sultan Adil Shah.

Following that, Sultan Adil Shah sent his forces along with some of his ministers to the Goa port to keep watch all the time and prevent the people of that place and other towns from supplying provisions to the Portuguese. Then, the Sultan sent his envoys to Adhraja, the Zamorin and Kolattiri with letters and gifts seeking their assistance in his campaign at Goa and blockade against the enemy. When the envoy arrived at Kollam with his entourage, Kolattiri's viceroy, who was also the third heir to the crown, arrested him and put him behind bars at the instigation of the Portuguese. The envoy somehow managed to escape from prison. Although Adhraja and Kolattiri himself asked him to return the presents and goods to the envoy, it was to no avail. His response was that he would have handed even the envoy over to the Portuguese had he not managed to escape from prison. All these took place in 986 AH (1578 AD).

The same year, some Portuguese officers approached the Zamorin and talked of peace with him. The Zamorin was then at the Hindu temple[a] of Kodungallur, which was held sacred by the non-believers of Malabar, and therefore it was here the Portuguese envoys met him in person. The Zamorin requested the Portuguese to build a fort in Calicut. Then the Portuguese wanted a fort to be built in Ponnani also but the Zamorin refused this request. The Zamorin sent along with the Portuguese

---

a. It was probably the Tirunavay temple.

officers, who came entreating for peace, three able and trustworthy persons to Goa to negotiate peace.[a] The Goa viceroy received them with great honour and respect. Then the envoys returned to Zamorin. But the negotiations fell through because the Portuguese insisted in building a port in Ponnani. This happened in 987 AH (1579 AD).

In the same year, peace was concluded between Adil Shah and Portuguese after they paid the Sultan a certain sum of money.

The Kochi king made preparations for war against the Zamorin for he wanted to turn him out of the temple mentioned above. He gathered a large group of men and then sent letters to the Portuguese viceroy at Goa seeking assistance in his war against the Zamorin. In response, the Portuguese viceroy delivered several war ships to him. All these joined together and fought against the Zamorin, who, in spite of his small army, was able, with the help of Allah, to defeat the Portuguese and the Kochi ruler. A large number of allied forces were killed and put to flight. The Zamorin and his men did not suffer any loss in spite of their small number.

Then the Portuguese continued to obstruct from Kochi the trade trips of the Muslims and capture their ships. May Allah forsake them and chastise them with a severe chastisement!

In the monsoon season of 990 or 991 AH (1582-83 AD) the Portuguese secretly mounted a vigil throughout the season against the subjects of the Zamorin from Calicut, Puttanangadi, Kakkad, Pantalayani, Tikkodi and Ponnani. These were territories under the rule of the Zamorin. This foiled the trade trips from these territories and even travels between the neighbouring towns became impossible for them. Thus the

---

a. The Portuguese Viceroy at Goa in 1578 AD was Don Diego de Menezes.

import of rice from Talnar (Talaimannar, Ramnad) also came to be disrupted. As a result, unprecedented poverty, famine and starvation occurred all over the country. All ports were under the control of the Portuguese and all import and export came to a stop. And besides, they were capturing every ship that passed by. What the Muslims could do except beseech Allah: "Our Lord! Rescue us from this town, whose people are oppressors; and raise for us from Thee one who will help protect us!"[7]

While things remained thus, the Portuguese once again, in the beginning of the trade season of 992 AH (1583 AD) attempted to have a treaty with the Zamorin. Finally they came to an agreement on the following terms: the Portuguese will be permitted to build a fort in Ponnani; the Portuguese captives in the hands of the Muslims will be handed over to the Portuguese viceroy and the Zamorin's subjects in the Portuguese captivity will be handed back to the Zamorin. Accordingly, the Muslims handed over the Portuguese captives with them to the Portuguese viceroy with immediate effect. The Muslim captives with the Portuguese were very few in number. The Portuguese handed them over to the Zamorin too. It was decided that the construction of the fort would start in the following year after the arrival of the new viceroy from Portugal.

The following year four ships arrived from Portugal in the beginning of the trade season. One of them had the new viceroy from Portugal aboard. Two of the ships harboured at Goa and the other two near Kollam. Following that, the then viceroy handed over the power to the new viceroy.

The new viceroy went straight to Goa without landing at Calicut, and therefore the Zamorin could not meet him nor could he present to him the gifts he had made ready for him. After the viceroy's arrival at Goa, the Zamorin sent a few dignitaries there. They met the viceroy, discussed matters and signed a new treaty.[8]

On the basis of the new treaty, the Zamorin's subjects resumed their trade trips to places like Gujarat as before. The same year, before the trade season was over, two ships with merchandise set out from Calicut to the Arabian shores.[9]

O Allah, the Most Merciful! Bring upon the Muslims a state of well-being. Everything is Your mercy! All Praises are due to You!

End Notes

Introduction

1. For the special treatment of the Prophet's family, blood relationship is not the only criterion. It is the purity of their nature and sacred station. Conceding greatness simply based on blood relationship does not agree with the spirit of the Holy Qur'an. "The noblest of you in the sight of Allah is the best in conduct" (Qur'an 49:13). n

2. The 'noblest of creations' (*ashraf al-khalq*) is an attribute of the Prophet Muḥammad (s). It is a divine bounty on him. Imām Aḥmad reports that the Prophet (s) said: "I have received what other messengers have not received." His disciples asked him what they were. He replied: "My enemies are afraid of me; I have received the keys of the earth; I have been named Aḥmad; soil has been made cleaning and purifying agent for me; and my community is superior to the rest of the communities."

3. First part of verse 100 of Sūrah Āl 'Imrān, in the Qur'an. The importance of enjoining right conduct and forbidding indecency and having firm faith in Allah—qualities and responsibilities of the ideal society—is further explained in the verse.

4. Imām al-Tirmidhī (r) has recorded this tradition (*ḥadīth*) in his Compilation quoting Abū Sa'īd al-Khudrī (r), a companion of the Prophet. The tradition in full is thus: "I will be the leader of all the children of Adam on the Day of Resurrection. This is not pride. The flag *al-ḥamd* will be in my hands. All the messengers will be behind the flag in my hands. I'll be the first to emerge from graves cleaving the earth. This is not talk of pride."

5. Imām Aḥmad bin Ḥanbal (164-241 AH) was born in Baghdad and his death also took place there. He was one of the six foremost scholars of Ḥadīth, an expert in Islamic jurisprudence and an eminent theologian. The Ḥanbalī school of Islamic jurisprudence is named after him. He had to serve a time in prison on account of his opposition to the Mu'tazilah sect. He travelled widely to Shām, Yemen, Ḥijāz, etc., for collecting Ḥadīth. His famous collection *Al-Musnad* contains thirty thousand *ḥādīth*.

6. Miqdād was one of the first seven who made public their faith in Islam. He was one of those who migrated to Ethiopia and took part in the battles of Badr and Uḥud. He was one of those whom the Prophet endeared greatly. He died in Madīnah in 33 AH.

7. Ibn Kathīr has quoted this *ḥadīth* in his *tafsīr* (interpretation) of verse 33 of Sūrah al-Tawbah of the Qur'an. The meaning of the verse is this: "It is He Who hath sent His Messenger with Guidance and the Religion of Truth, to proclaim it over all religion, even though the Pagans may detest (it)." This is an indication that a time will come afterwards when all sections of the society come under Islam and live accordingly. Imām Aḥmad (r) reports from Tamīm al-Dārī (r), a companion of the Prophet (s): "I heard the Prophet (s) saying: 'This religion will reach wherever night and day reach. No mansion or hut will be spared from its reach. Thus there will be those who get dignified by embracing Islam and those who continue in their wretchedness by remaining in their disbelief.' Tamīm al-Dārī (r) recalls that he could see afterwards instances of both cases in his own family. Those who embraced Islam could achieve dignity and well-being and the disbelievers had to live subdued paying the *jizyah* tax."

8. The history of the spread of Islam in various parts of the world including India is clearly documented. It may be noted here that Sir Thomas Arnold, in his famous work *The Preaching of Islam*, has given very clear, effective and incontrovertible reply to those who keep saying that Islam was spread with sword. Arnold has further explained the real reasons why Islam spread widely all over the world.

9. Malabar means a territory of hills and mountains. The word here is not merely suggestive of Malabar today. It rather includes the whole of modern Kerala. The Malabar in the map with the Arab geographers is the territory extending from Gokarnam to Kanyakumari. Foreigners, even today, use the word Malabar to mean Kerala as a whole.

10. The rulers of this place had the tolerance and broadmindedness to receive the followers of other religions, recognise them and facilitate them to propagate their faith even while they kept faith in their religion, adhered to it in life and were committed to it. This might be because of their piety and sense of justice that enjoin them to honour truth and values wholeheartedly, or because of the warm relationship they had with the nations from where propagators of other religions arrived or even because of the personality, purity, manners and exemplary life that they could witness in the propagators.

11. The self-critical approach of Shaykh Zainuddin is noteworthy. Even when he describes the Portuguese invasion and their atrocities, he does not leave unnoticed the role the condition of his community then had in having to undergo that experience. He views the Portuguese invasion as a divine punishment for the deviation of the Muslims from the right path. Verses 4-8 of

the Sūrah al-Isrā' in the Qur'an that refer to the experience of the Israelites, as when they began a life of transgression and deviation as a prophetic society, of being divinely punished by being put to the oppressive rule of Nebuchadnezzar and others, their persecution and torture, and their demolition of the Jerusalem temple, could be recalled in this context.

12. The period of the Portuguese occupation in Malabar was from 1498 to 1663 AD. The author finished writing the book in 1583, and in the same year the sad demise of the author took place. Therefore, only eighty five years' Portuguese reign is being discussed in this book.

13. The Muslims had been urged to fight the Portuguese not because they were worshippers of cross, but because they were invaders, oppressors and intruders. Although worship of cross is a sin and great transgression in the perspective of Islam, it is a religious rite for the Christians.

14. Adil Shah was one of the five independent Muslim dynasties in the southern India. Adil Shah dynasty came into prominence by the decline of the Bahmanid kings. This dynasty was founded in 1489 AD by Yusuf Adil Shah who came from Persia. The Adil Shah kings who liberally encouraged art and literature had an allegiance to the Imāmiyyah Ithnā 'Ashariyyah section of the Shi'ite movement. Ali Adil Shah I was the fifth king of this dynasty. The period of his reign was from 1557 to 1580 Ad. Ali Adil Shah who recaptured many of the territories lost during the reign of his father Ibrahim Adil Shah is quite famous in history. That Shaykh Zainuddin who was a famous Sunni scholar talks about Ali Adil Shah, a famous Shi'ite king, with great admiration, and dedicates his book to him, is quite surprising. This is an exemplary attitude of tolerance to be imitated by scholars of all sections of all time.

15. *Jinns* are a unique creation different from human beings, with intelligence and great capacity for action. It is believed that this species, invisible to man, appears before them taking the shape of human beings and creatures like dog, snake, etc. That the *jinns* wanted to serve Ali Adil Shah is either an exaggeration or a metaphorical description.

Section One

1. The Arabic word *kuffār*, plural of *kāfir* is translated 'unbelievers' here. The context here is that of the Muslim territories being invaded by the Portuguese. Therefore, the author is explaining the attitude to be taken towards those invading non-believers. This is not the strategy to be followed during peacetime, nor is it the general policy and strategy the Muslims are supposed to adopt, or had adopted in the historical past, towards non-Muslims. It should also be remembered here that the Zamorin, a non-Muslim ruler, and his Nair forces, were with the Muslims in their struggle against the Portuguese.

2. *Jihād* is an Arabic word. It means struggle, effort, and sacrifice, etc. Although all these might be something undertaken by a military force, one cannot translate the word precisely as 'military campaign' or 'holy war'. Even if this word is used to suggest war, it is not the ordinary war that it implies. That is why this word is an exclusive technical term of Islam. In Arabic, the word usually used for war is *ḥarb*. The word *ijtihād*, suggestive of intellectual and epistemological efforts in research, and *jihād*, are from the common root *jahada*. The struggle taking place in one's soul and mind also could be suggested by the word *jihād*. In short, *jihād* is a conflict between two opposite forces, or tendencies. It need not be an armed struggle. It could be an armed struggle as well. There can be *jihād* between two ideologies: ideological conflicts. What Islam postulates by *jihād* is a holistic concept, not war. *Jihād* is acceptable and allowed in Islam only if it is in the path of Allah. And what is Allah's path is very clearly explained in the Qur'an and Ḥadīth.

3. The technical term for collective responsibility in Islam is *farḍ kifāyah*.

4. The term for individual responsibility is *farḍ 'ayn*.

5. The author is here explaining an issue in Islamic jurisprudence, and not because slavery was prevalent in the Muslim society at the time of writing this book.

6. The author has estimated this distance in his renowned book *Fatḥ al-Mu'īn* to the distance covered by a man on camel with reasonably heavy luggage during a period of one night and one day only stopping for the basic requirements such as prayer, food and rest.

7. Aḥmad and al-Shāfi' (r) have reported from Abū Hurayrah that he had not seen anybody discussing matters with the followers better than the Prophet (s). Discussion with others and developing consensus are very important not only in matters concerning war but in all walks of life. The Prophet (s) who had been guided by divine inspiration and revelation did so not because he was in need of the advice and suggestions of his followers but to teach this great human value.

8. Things captured from enemies as spoils of war are called *ghanīmah* or *nafal*. This includes the captured land as well as human captives. Verse 41 of Sūrah al-Anfāl in the Qur'an describes the distribution of the spoils of war.

9. *Qāḍī* and *Imām* are those who lead the Muslims in their regular prayers and give leadership to them in all religious matters. The mosques are their headquarters. Since their life is fully dedicated to the service of the society, it is the collective responsibility of the society to protect them.

10. Hāshim, the great-grandfather of Prophet Muḥammad (s), was the son of 'Abd Manāf. He was a man of great consequence as well as riches among the Quraysh. He was the receiver of the tax imposed on the Qurayshites by

Qūṣay for the support of the pilgrims, and the income derived from their contributions joined to his own resources, was employed in providing food to the strangers who congregated at Makkah during the season of the pilgrimage.

Like the majority of the people of Makkah, Hāshim was engaged in commerce. It was he who founded among the Qurayshites the custom of sending out regularly from Makkah two caravans, one in winter to Yemen, and the other in summer to Syria. Hāshim died in the course of one of his expeditions to Syria, in the city of Ghazza about the year 510 AD.

'Abd al-Muṭṭalib was the only son of Hāshim, by a Yathribite lady of the name of Salmah. His original name was Shaybah. Muṭṭalib, the brother of Hāshim, brought Shaybah, the white-haired youth, from Yathrib to Makkah. Mistaking Shaybah for a slave of Muṭṭalib, the people of Makkah called him 'Abd al-Muṭṭalib and history recognises the grandfather of the Prophet under no other name than that of 'Abd al-Muṭṭalib, 'the slave of Muṭṭalib'.

After the death of Muṭṭalib at Kazwan, in Yemen, towards the end of 520 AD 'Abd al-Muṭṭalib succeeded him as the head of the Commonwealth of Makkah.

'Abd al-Muṭṭalib had ten sons and six daughters. Of the sons (1) Ḥārith, born towards 538 AD was the eldest. The others were (2) 'Abd al-'Uzzā, alias Abū Lahab, (3) 'Abd Manāf better known as Abū Ṭālib (died in 620 AD, (4) Zubayr, (5) 'Abdullah (545 AD), born of Fāṭimah, daughter of 'Amr; (6) Ḍirār; (7) 'Abbās (566-652) born of Nutaylah; (8) Mukawwim; (9) Jahm; and (10) Ḥamzah, born of Hālah.

The daughters were 'Ātikah, Umaymah, Arwā, Barrah, and Umm Ḥakīm, by Fāṭimah; and Ṣafiyah, born of Hālah, who married 'Awwām, the grandfather of the famous 'Abdullah bin Zubayr, who played such an important part in the history of Islam.

It is also said that 'Abd al-Muṭṭalib had twelve sons. But the names of the two sons, other than the sons mentioned above, are not known, probably because they left no posterity.[Nainar]

11. If ever anything belonging to the spoils of war has been found in the illegal possession of anybody, the rule is to flog him and to burn everything in his possession. There was an incident of the Prophet (s) declining to offer the prayer after death for one who had illegally taken a trifle from among the spoils of war.

12. Zamorin ('Samuri' in the Arabic text of the book; pronounced 'Samootiri' in Malayalam, the local language) was the common title of the rulers of Calicut during the middle age. The origin and early history of the Zamorins of Calicut are shrouded in mystery. We do not hear of the Zamorin before the days of Abdul-Razzaq (1442). The political condition of Malabar before the commencement of the sixteenth century presents an interesting study. The whole country between Cannanore and Cape Comorin consisted of a number of petty principalities under princelings who were very often waging war against one another. The principal rulers in the area were the king of Cannanore, the

Zamorin or the king of Calicut and the Tiruvidi or the king Vayanad, to whom the smaller rulers paid allegiance. They were entitled to wear the crown, issue coins and use the ceremonial umbrella. The Zamorin was of Nair caste. Though his authority was questioned by the Raja of Valluvanad prior to the thirteenth century, he became later the most important ruler of the west coast wielding much influence and power. When the Portuguese came to India, the Zamorin was very powerful as compared with the Raja of Cochin.

The origin of the word *Samuri* has been a puzzle to scholars. Some consider it to be a word derived from Persian or Arabic, while some consider that it is derived from the contracted compound of the Sanskrit Suami and Tirumalpad. (K.V. Krishna Ayyar, *The Zamorins of Calicut*, pp. 13-15) But it is more probable that it is shortened from the title *Samudragiriraja* meaning 'lord of hills and waves'. The Zamorin had also another title, *Kunnalkkonatiri*, meaning 'king of hills and waves'. These names indicated the important position the Zamorin held on the west coast.

Another opinion, in fact a far fetched, is that the name Zamorin probably came from the word Samiri, the name of one Samiri in the story of Mūsā (as). He had persuaded the followers of Mūsā (as) in his absence to worship the image of a calf he had made. The Arabs who came to notice his cow worship called him Samiri which later on became Zamorin. It was Koyilkota, the name of the palace of the Zamorins that later on became Kozhikode (Calicut). During the hundred years of struggle with the Portuguese, fifteen Zamorins ruled over the area in succession. Some were powerful and charismatic and some others were weak. Some even joined the Portuguese side.

13. It is the collective responsibility of the Muslims to recapture their territory occupied by the enemies. If nobody undertakes this responsibility, all will be sinful and answerable for the omission. If ever anybody undertakes it, it means that he is doing a great service by absolving the rest of the community of the sin of collective negligence.

14. Angels are a special creation of Allah, created from light. They do not experience hunger or thirst, sleep, drowsiness or boredom. They have no sex difference, and may appear in the shape of any except the filthy, wretched animals. They do nothing but praise and obey Allah.

15. The reference here is to *awliyā'*, those among the believers who attained a high level of spirituality. It is the plural of the Arabic word *walī*, which means one who is close, near, etc. One becomes a *walī* when the veil between his heart and Allah vanishes. There is a reference to such people in verses 62-64 of Sūrah Yūnus in the Qur'an.

16. This is Muslim bin al-Ḥajjāj alias Abu al-Ḥusayn al-Qushayrī al-Naysabūrī. His compilation of Ḥadīth, *al-Ṣaḥīḥ*, is quite well known. Besides Muslim, this *hadīth* has been documented by al-Ṭabrānī and al-Tirmidhī, two other Ḥadīth compilers.

17. Sūrah al-Nisā': 75. The historical context of the verse is that of enjoining the Muslims to fight for the weak among them waiting for a liberator when they were being incessantly tortured and oppressed in Makkah. Liberation of the oppressed is one of the supreme goals of war in Islam.

18. Sūrah al-Baqarah: 216.
The Muslims are neither desirous of war, nor cowards. At the time, about the revelation of the above mentioned verse, they had to think seriously about two things: one, the general condition of the Muslims was not quite suitable for a confrontation then. Their enemies were in a much better position in every respect. They were more powerful, in terms of their number, wealth etc. It would be much better for them to consider a confrontation after a considerable improvement in the situation. A confrontation in the present stage will not bring any favourable outcome for them. Secondly, the humanitarian disposition of mind that Islam nurtured was not one that encourages war. The enemies are also human beings. They are also creations of Allah. Instead of engaging them in a war, they are to be persuaded to come closer to the path of Allah by means of affectionate behaviour and sympathetic attitudes. But what Allah taught them at this stage is that both these concerns are out of context and they seem important to them only because they do not know how things are going to turn out finally. This is what is suggested by the verse: "Allah knows and you do not know."
It is not cowardice, but the two concerns explained above, that makes war hateful to the Muslims. Yet, in any society of brave people, there might be a few who are weak and cowardly. Their cowardice, sometimes, may affect them all. And there might have been a few of this kind in the society of the Prophet (s) also. The verse cited above might be a reproach on such people as well.

19. Sūrah al-Tawbah: 111. The covenant between Allah and the believers is compared with a trade here. Allah is the buyer and the believers are the sellers. The life and the wealth of the believers are the merchandise. The paradise is the price or reward. The Torah, the Gospel, and the Qur'an are the witnesses for the deal.

20. Sūrah al-Baqarah: 261. Any kind of spending aiming the pleasure, satisfaction and nearness of Allah will be treated as spending in the cause of Allah. The author has quoted this line here in encouragement for spending one's wealth for supporting *jihād*.

21. Sūrah Āl 'Imrān: 169-170. Those who are living in the presence of Allah, have no reason to feel fear or grief. These verses make clear that the martyrs in the cause of Allah have no death.

22. Muḥammad bin Ismā'īl (194-256 AH), better known as al-Bukhārī, was a renowned compiler of Ḥadīth, historian and great scholar of Islamic jurisprudence. Born in Bukhara, western Uzbekistan, he travelled widely in many countries searching for and studying the Ḥadīth. He died at Kartank in

Samarqand. Books that have documented only *aḥādīth* which have been verified and proved genuine and true, are known as *Ṣaḥīḥ*. Six such genuine collections—*Al-Jāmiʿ al-Ṣaḥīḥ* by al-Bukhārī, *al-Ṣaḥīḥ* by Muslim, *Sunan* by Abū Dāwūd, *Jāmiʿ* by al-Tirmidhī, *Sunan* by al-Nasāʾī and *Sunan* by Ibn Mājah—are widely known as *Al-Siḥaḥ al-Sittah*.

23. Abū Hurayrah is another name by which the Prophet's companion ʿAbd al-Raḥmān was known.

24. As the problems of the early community of Islam became more complex, it was usual in theological circles to imagine what the practice (*sunnah*) of the Prophet would have been under each new set of circumstances and pass their judgement into circulation as a tradition (*ḥadīth*) emanating from the Prophet himself. These judgements swayed by the conflicting views of sects and parties were naturally often in open contraction. As there were no written records or compilations of the *ḥadīth*, the students of Ḥadīth faced with the necessity of discriminating between them, fixed their attention first on the authenticity of the chain of authority (*isnād*) by which the tradition was supported. They held that every tradition must be guaranteed by some reliable person as having been received by him from some other reliable person who himself had heard it from an earlier traditionist and so on back to a contemporary of the Prophet who vouched for having heard the Prophet saying the words or seen him doing the action related therein. In the nature of it the chain of authorities (*isnād*) could as easily be forged as a tradition; and so, for two centuries every movement in Islam attempted to gain support for its action by putting into the mouth of the Prophet utterances in favour of its views.

In these circumstances it became imperative to establish a corpus of traditions which could be accepted as genuine. The traditionists who insured on the *isnād* criterion, eventually came to a general agreement that only certain chains of transmission could be regarded as authoritative. It was on these principles Abū ʿAbdullah Muḥammad bin Ismāʿīl al-Bukhārī and Abu al-Ḥusayn bin al-Ḥajjāj Muslim selected their traditions out of several hundred thousand and gave the name *Ṣaḥīḥ* (authoritative) to their collections.

Abū ʿAbdullah Muḥammad bin Ismāʿīl al-Bukhārī was born at Bukhara on 21 July, 810 AD, of a Persian family. When he was in his teens, he went on a pilgrimage to Makkah, and took this opportunity to attend lectures given by teachers of the tradition at Makkah and Madīnah. He then went to Egypt, and travelled with the same object all over Muslim world, spending five whole years at Basra. After an absence of sixteen years in all, he returned to Bukhara and there he compiled his *Ṣaḥīḥ*. He died on 30 August, 870 AD.

Abu al-Ḥusayn bin al-Ḥajjāj Muslim was born at Nishapur in Khurasan in 817 AD. He went to the Ḥijāz, Iraq, Syria and Egypt in order to search out *aḥādīth*. He also paid several visits to Baghdad. He is said to have collected more than three hundred thousand *aḥādīth*, on which his selection is based. The matter of Muslim's book, like that contained in al-Bukhārī's (with which it is identical, except for the addition of more authorities) is arranged in the order adopted for legal subjects, but without any chapter headings. It is also remarkable for its introduction, wherein the author treats of the science of Ḥadīth in a general and complete manner.

The *Ṣaḥīḥs* of Bukhārī and Muslim have become two canonical books of Islam. They may be considered to sum up the science of Ḥadīth in the third century of the Hijrah. Four other works complete the six canonical books to which Muslims pay great respect. They were all produced during the same period. These are the *Sunan* of Abū Dāwūd, the *Jāmi'* of Abū 'Īsā Muḥammad al-Tirmidhī, the *Sunan* of Abū 'Abd al-Raḥmān Aḥmad al-Nasā'ī, and the *Sunan* of Abū 'Abdullah Muḥammad bin Mājah. [Nainar]

25. *Jihād* aims at the survival and development of the religion of Islam and humanity. It is unavoidable for the survival of the truth. Therefore, whenever it becomes necessary, *jihād* is of uppermost significance after faith (*imān*). The essential vitality of all kinds of worships is present in *jihād*. It is renouncement of all bodily interests and worldly aspirations and a spiritual journey to Allah sacrificing everything including one's life and wealth.

26. The implication of *jihād* here is the armed struggle to uphold the ideals of religion. That is why it has been translated here 'holy struggle'; and it is not necessarily an accurate translation.

27. There is a sentence to this effect in the *Ṣaḥīḥ* of Bukhārī. The Prophet (s) did not personally take part in some of the military expeditions during his time. He sent the forces under the most efficient among his followers. The reason for this is explained here. Even as the one gifted with the highest position of the final Prophet (s), he aspired for martyrdom.

28. The Prophet (s) spoke so after having said three times that one will not find anything equal to *jihād* in answer to the question as to what was equal to *jihād*. One has to bear in mind that the reward for the prayers and other virtuous deeds of one in the course of *jihād* will be an addition.

29. Similar *ḥadīths* can be found in al-Bukhārī's *Ṣaḥīḥ* and Aḥmad's *Musnad*. The musk smelling blood is a surreal description. The greatness of martyrdom makes that blood sacred and glorious.

30. Anas bin Mālik alias Abū Ḥamzah al-Anṣārī (r) was born ten years before Hijrah. Anas, who lived as the Prophet's servant from Hijrah until the demise of the Prophet (s), has reported many *aḥādīth* (1286). He had advised his children to keep the *aḥādīth* documented in writing. He used to say: "the undocumented information will not be treated credible." He died at Basrah in 93 AH.

31. This *ḥadīth* is in the *Sunan* of Ibn Mājah (r). By this phrase—in the cause of Allah—*jihād* is implied. The virtue of spending just one morning or one evening in the cause of *jihād* is described here.

32. Al-Bukhārī (r) reports this *ḥadīth*.

33. There are three probable persons referred to here: Jābir bin 'Abdullah bin 'Amr al-Sulamī (r), Jābir bin 'Abdullah al-Bajālī (r) and Jābir bin Samurah bin Junādah al-'Āmirī (r). Which Jābir is meant here is not clear. Bajālī had not taken part in the battle of Uḥud. There are not many *aḥādīth* (just 146) reported by 'Āmirī. He died in Madīnah after he was seventy. He had taken part in 17 battles together with the Prophet (s).

34. The battle of Uḥud is the one that took place on mount Uḥud , three miles from Madīnah, in the third year of Hijrah between the Prophet (s) and the polytheists of Makkah.

35. Sahl bin Sa'd al-Saydī (r) was a companion of the Prophet (s) who was born nine years before Hijrah and died in 91 AH.

36. This is reported in the *Ṣaḥīḥ* of Bukhārī. The greatness of the virtue of those who volunteer to keep vigil and guard the border is proportionate to the risky and critical nature of the responsibility.

37. 'Abdullah bin Qays alias Abū Mūsā al-Asha'rī (r) was a well known companion of the Prophet (s). It was he who represented 'Alī (r), the fourth caliph, in the peace talk following the battle of Ṣiffīn between 'Alī (r) and Mu'āwiyah in 37 AH. He died in Kufah in 44 AH.

38. This *ḥadīth* is in the *Sunan* of Abū Dāwūd. Whoever fights aspiring worldly gains, although he is doing so as part of the Islamic force, will not be a fighter in the cause of Allah. Muslim has reported a *ḥadīth* from Abū Hurayrah to the effect that one who died fighting for honour and fame will be hurled into hell following interrogation in the Hereafter. Sincere intentions make a man's deeds and sacrifices valuable in the Hereafter.

39. Sa'd bin Mālik al-Khazrajī alias Abū Sa'īd al-Khudrī (r) was an important companion of the Prophet (s) and a great scholar who had memorised a number of *aḥādīth*. There are 1,170 *aḥādīth* reported from him.

40. The *ḥadīth* quoted here is in *Kanz al-'Ummāl fī Sunan al-Af'āl wal-Aqwāl*, the compilation of *aḥādīth* by 'Allāmah 'Alā'uddīn 'Alī al-Muttaqī bin Ḥusāmuddīn al-Hindī. Only a portion of the *ḥadīth* is given here. The *ḥadīth* contains answers to the questions as to who are the good among the people and who are the bad.

41. This is in the *Ṣaḥīḥ* of Bukhārī. *Firdaws* is the Arabic word for paradise. The word appears in verses 18:107 and 23:11of the Qur'an.

42. The real name of Abū 'Abs bin Jabar (r) was 'Abd al-Raḥmān. A member of the Aws tribe, he was one of the important companions of the Prophet (s). He took part in all the battles of Islam during the time of the Prophet (s)

including Badr. It was he who led the prayer after death (*janāzah*) for 'Uthmān (r). He was seventy when he died in 34 AH.

43. There are statements to this effect in the *hadīth* compilations of al Bukhārī and al-Nasā'ī.

44. The author has not made clear which Sa'd he means here. Sa'd bin Mu'ādh (r), Sa'd bin 'Ubādah (r), Sa'd bin 'Ubayd (r), or Sa'd bin Abī Waqqāṣ (r)? The first battle of Islam was Badr. Sa'd bin Mu'ādh had actively taken part in this battle. He was martyred following the injury he sustained from an arrow shot at him during the battle of Khandaq. Sa'd bin 'Ubayd (r) and Sa'd bin Abī Waqqāṣ (r) also had taken part in the battle of Badr. It is doubtful whether Sa'd bin 'Ubādah (r) had participated in the battle of Badr. Since Sa'd bin Abī Waqqāṣ was the best known of them as an archer, the Sa'd mentioned here is likely to be none other than him. Likewise, the author has not made clear the identity of Abū Qays who heard Sa'd. Who was he, Abū Qays bin Ṣirmah (r), Abū Qays bin Mualla (r), Abū Qays Juhani (r), Abū Qays bin Ḥārith (r) or Abū Qays al-Anṣārī (r), or somebody else?

45. This is described in both *al-Bukhārī* and *Muslim*.

46. This *hadīth* reported by al-Bukhārī implies that even the silliest remainders of the things used for waging a war in the cause of Allah increase the glory and virtue of the fighter.

47. The *hadīth* has also been included in the *Sunan* of Abū Dāwūd. How can one be sure of one's commitment to his faith if he does not take part in the *jihād* when the occasion demands it, or does not wish to take part in it or at least regret for not being able to do so? Hypocrisy and sincerity are separated through a process of severe tests. This is the meaning of the verse (47:31) in the Qur'an: "And We shall try you until We test those among you who strive their utmost and persevere in patience..."

48. The *hadīth* quoted here could be seen in the Ḥadīth compilation *Kanz al-'Ummāl*. Such statements are meant for motivating the Muslims to bravely participate in the struggle against the unbelievers if war breaks out. It does not mean that Muslims will be automatically admitted into heaven for killing the non-believers on any occasion. Interpreting things in such a way is nothing but an insult to the spirit of Islam.

49. This *hadīth* is reported in *Kanz al-'Ummāl* and Aḥmad's *Musnad*. Its first portion praises the life of a soldier who fights on horseback. The last portion might appear to encourage life in seclusion, away from the society. But all messengers, majority of the companions of the Prophet (s) and most of the great scholars of Islam lived fully involved in society. A soldier for truth is one who is eager to lay down his life for the pleasure of Allah, in the cause of the truth and the society. The second person is one who abandons the people for

realising truth. The meaning of this line could be understood comprehensively only by viewing them both in two different contexts, in two different fields.

50. Jābir bin Samurah bin Junada al-Amīrī (r) was the nephew of Sa'd bin Abī Waqqāṣ (r). There are 146 *aḥādīth* included in the compilations reported by this great companion of the Prophet (s). He died in Kufah in 74 AH at the age of seventy.

51. This is a historical fact. There were many to fight for Islam in all ages. There was not a single time in history when there was nobody to fight for Islam.

52. Salmān (r), born in an aristocratic family in Isfahan, Persia, was one of the close companions of the Prophet (s). The Prophet has described him even as "a member of his family". Salmān (r) was a man of strenuous and diligent nature and was known for his generosity. He was also known for his war strategies. Eminent companions of the Prophet (s) like Abū Hurayrah (r) and Ibn 'Abbās (r) have reported several *aḥādīth* from him. He died in 35 AH.

53. This *ḥadīth* was reported by Muslim. The implication of the statement that a ready feast is sure for the one who dies while keeping vigil is that he will be one of the martyrs who live in the presence of Allah being generously fed. The implication of the last sentence is that he will not have to undergo any difficulty while in grave or anywhere else.

54. 'Uqbah bin 'Āmir (r) was a well known companion of the Prophet (s) belonging to the Khazraj tribe. He was governor of Egypt for a time and was buried in the al-Muwattam hill near Cairo.

55. Both the *ḥadīths* quoted here are included in *Kanz al-'Ummāl* and *Ṣaḥīḥ* of Muslim. The importance of archery is underscored in the first *ḥadīth* in explanation to the verse (8:60), "Against them (your enemies) make ready your strength to the utmost of your power..." The Prophet used to give utmost encouragement to his followers to get trained in archery, martial arts, and horse riding.

56. The actual name Abū Mas'ūd al-Anṣārī was 'Uqbah bin 'Amr al-Badrī (r).

57. This *ḥadīth* is included in *Sunan* of al-Dārimī. The real name of this great scholar of Ḥadīth was 'Abdullah Abū Muḥammad al-Tamīmī. He was born in Samarqand and died in 255 AH. The implication of the *ḥadīth* here is that whatever one spends in the cause of the struggle in the path of Allah will be rewarded in the hereafter multiplied seven hundred times.

58. When Abū 'Ā'ishah Masrūq bin al-Ajda' embraced Islam, he accepted the new name 'Abd al-Raḥmān. He was a Yemeni. Although he was a contemporary of the Prophet (s) for a period, his embrace of Islam took place only during the reign of Abū Bakr. Therefore, he was not a companion of the Prophet. He died in 63 AH.

59. 'Abdullah bin Mas'ūd al-Hudalī (r) was the sixth to embrace Islam in Makkah and was the first of those who recited the Qur'an aloud publicly.

60. Ibn Mājah and al-Dārimī report this *hadīth* in their *Musnads*. The glory of the martyrs that rises even to the altitude of the divine throne is described here. The appearance and disappearance of Allah is a supra sensory experience. It need not be a bodily vision. What is described here is an experience in the metaphysical or supernatural world.

61. 'Abdullah (r) was son of 'Amr bin al-'Āṣ (r), the famous Arab military leader and companion of the Prophet (s).

62. This *hadīth* is in Aḥmad's *Musnad*. Since debt is a responsibility between human individuals, the right to exonerate the borrower from it is with the lender.

63. The battle of Badr was fought between the Muslims and the Quraysh in January 624 AD. A force consisting of a thousand well-equipped men under the noted Abū Jahl, 'the Father of Ignorance', marched out from Makkah to relieve a rich caravan. The Muslims received timely notice of the movement and a body of three hundred disciples proceeded at once to forestall the heathens by occupying the valley of Badr, upon which the Quraysh, under Abū Jahl, were moving. A battle ensued. The Quraysh fought bravely. At one time the fortunes of the field wavered, but Muḥammad's appeal to his people decided the fate of the battle. The Quraysh were driven back with great loss; many of their chiefs were slain, including Abū Jahl. But the importance of the Prophet's success cannot be measured by the material damage which he inflicted. Considering the momentous issues involved, Badr, like Marathon, or Plassey is one of the greatest and most memorable battles in all history. The victory of Badr turned all eyes upon Muḥammad. He became a power in Arabia. [Nainar]

64. In verse 133 of Sūrah Āl 'Imrān in the Qur'an, the heaven is described to be as wide as the skies and the earths. It means that it is as wide as the universe. The statement is descriptive of the vastness of heaven. Vastness is relief and comfort. Narrowness is uncomfortable and difficult. This verse is to be understood in this sense.

65. This description is found in al-Nasā'ī's *Sunan*. It could be seen in history that 'Umayr (r) had said to the effect that he was obstructed from reaching heaven because of their delay in killing him. This was 'Umayr bin al-Humām bin al-Jamūḥ bin al-Ḥarām. He was the first to be martyred from among the Anṣārs (those who hosted the Prophet in Madīnah).

66. Fuḍālah bin 'Ubayd (r) was an important companion of the Prophet (s) and an expert in the art of the Qur'an recitation.

67. Abū Umāmah Suda' bin 'Ajalān (r) was an important companion of the Prophet (s) and a well-known warrior.

68. What this sentence teaches is that if a person, at a time when *jihād* is crucial for the survival of Muslim society, keeps away from the struggle for the cause of Islam, not involving in it by any means, for selfish motives or for living comfortably, he deserves the wrath of Allah in this world itself.

69. 'Imrān bin Ḥusayn Abū Najīd al-Qusay (r) embraced Islam in the year of the battle of Khaybar. 'Umar (r), the second caliph of Islam, sent him to Basrah to teach the people there the principles and rites of Islam. He was the judge (*qāḍī*) of Basrah for a period. He did not join any side in the conflict between 'Alī (r) and Mu'āwiyah (r). Eventually, he was of the opinion that it was better withdrawing to the mountains and living there shepherding and in worship than being involved in political disputes. He died in 52 AH in Basrah.

70. The *hadīth* quoted here is in *Sunan* of Abū Dāwūd. Al-Dajjāl is a major evil force. The common belief of Muslims in this connection is that 'Īsā, or Jesus (a.s.) will appear in the final days and destroy al-Dajjāl. There are several *ahādīth* that describe the features of this evil force.

71. 'Abdullah (r), son of the Prophet's uncle al-'Abbās (r), was born three years before Hijrah. He was extremely intelligent and studious. There are 2,660 *ahādīth* reported from him. He died in 68 AH.

72. This *hadīth* is in *Nayl al-Awtar*, vol. vii.

73. *Aṣḥāb*, plural of *Ṣāḥib*, the Companions or Associates of Muḥammad. The term, used for a single Companion, is *ṣaḥābah*. There is considerable controversy as to who is to be regarded a Companion, and what elements make up this definition. Strictly speaking the term 'Companionship', in relation to the Prophet (s), can be attributed only to those personalities from among the earliest Muslims who were on intimate terms with him and shared his daily life, and, in varying degrees, also to his thoughts; that is to those who could be called friends in the deepest meaning of the word. But Muslim historians and theologians, have, from the third century of the Hijrah onward, begun to enlarge this term in a manner to include in it every person, who while being a Muslim, saw the Prophet (s) even without nearer association. [Nainar]

74. A *hadīth* to this effect in meaning is found quoted in al-Ḥākim's *al-Mustadrak*. The opportunities for the struggle against evil are present in social life. Life in aloofness might give opportunities for spiritual elevation, but an individual, in such cases in disregarding social responsibilities, forfeits all opportunities for his mental growth.

75. A person who gladly hugs martyrdom experiences the death pain only very lightly as he is in his dreams about the heavenly experiences.

76. This might be the Anṣārī companion of the Prophet (s) named Ḥarām bin al-Ḥukaym bin Khālid bin Sa'd bin al-Ḥakam (r).

77. This *ḥadīth* is in *Mustadrak al-Ṣaḥīḥayn.*

78. 'Alī (r), son of the Prophet's uncle Abū Ṭālib and husband of his daughter Fāṭimah al-Zahrā' (r), 'Alī (r) was the fourth caliph of Islam.

79. Uwaymir (r) better known as Abū al-Dardā' was a companion of the Prophet from the Khazraj tribe. His father was Mālik and mother Maḥabba. He was a good scholar of the Qur'an and reporter of several *aḥādīth*. He was *imām* and judge (*qāḍī*) in the Syrian capital Damascus during the reign of 'Uthmān (r). He died in 32 or 33 AH.

80. 'Abdullah (r), son of the second caliph 'Umar bin al-Khaṭṭāb (r), was born ten years before Hijrah. His mother was Zaynab. He was a very pious man. He reported 2,630 *aḥādīth* from the Prophet (s). He was very careful about quoting the words of the Prophet (s) textually leaving no room for any deviation in meaning. He kept away from politics, without involving in it, during crises and differences. Yet, he once reproached Ḥajjāj, the Umayyad ruler, in the presence of thousands of people. He died in Makkah in 73 AH. It is said that his death was caused by somebody, at the behest of Ḥajjāj, thrusting a poisoned spear on his foot while in a crowd.

81. This *ḥadīth* is in the compilations of Ibn Mājah and al-Nasā'ī.

82. A *ḥadīth* to this effect can be found in *Sunan* of Abū Dāwūd. The verse mentioned here is Sūrah Āl 'Imrān: 169, in the Qur'an.

83. Muḥammad bin Muḥammad bin Aḥmad bin Isḥāq, better known as al-Ḥākim, was born in Nisapur, capital of the Iranian province Khurasan in 290 AH. He is widely known as *"Baḥr al-'Ulūm"* (ocean of knowledge). His work *al-Mustadrak* is a famous compilation of *aḥādīth*. He died in 378 AH.

84. This is also included in *Ṣaḥīḥ* of Bukhārī.

85. Sulaymān bin Aḥmad bin Ayyūb Abū al-Qāsim al-Laqmī, better known as al-Ṭabarānī, was born in 'Akkah in Palestine in 260 AH. His works *Dalā'il al-Nubuwwah, Kitāb al-Awa'il, Mukhtaṣaru Makārim al-Akhlāq,* and *Al-Awsaṭ* are quite famous. He died in 360 AH.

86. The author has not made clear the identity of the person concerned here. This might be any one of these: a) Wāi'lah bin Masin Sa'sa'(r), b) Wāi'lah bin 'Amr bin Sha'bān al-Fihrī (r), c) Wāi'lah bin Tamsan bin Oud (r).

87. This *ḥadīth* is in *Kanz al-'Ummāl,* and *Sunan* of al-Nasā'ī and Ibn Mājah. Fighting at sea is more difficult, riskier and demands greater bravery than fighting on land. The meaning of the statement is that the reward for fighting at sea for the cause of Islam in the absence of the Prophet (s) is as great and glorious as the reward for fighting along with the Prophet (s). It has been explained in other *aḥādīth* that the martyrdom at sea is twice equal to

martyrdom on land and that martyrs at sea will even be exonerated from their debts.

88. Daylam is a mountain range in the Jeelan region of Persia. The famous scholar of *aḥādīth* Aḥmad bin Shīrawaihi bin Shahardan bin Shīrawaihi Abū Muslim Hamadānī, who was better known as al-Daylamī, was known after this place. He died in 625 AH.

Section Two

1. Kodungallur was known by different names such as Muchira, Musiris, and Mahodayapuram. It is a town in Trichur district in Kerala, south India. The advent of Christians and Jews to Kodungallur did not take place at the same time in history. Only that the author has described together the two events of two different epochs. It could be seen in history that a few Jews came here as refugees under the leadership of the rabbi Joseph after the fall of Jerusalem and that they were allowed to live here. But there is no consensus as to when and from where Jews arrived here first. Some say that it was during the time of the Prophet Sulaymān (a.s.) (King Solomon). There are documents that prove that the first arrival of Christians in Kerala happened in 52 AD. History observes that St. Thomas, disciple of Jesus, arrived at Kodungallur by a trade ship that year and began, for the first time, the propagation of Christianity in India. Yet there are quite a number of disputes over this due to the chronological discrepancies. It is said that Palli Bana Perumal gave him permission for the propagation of Christianity and for building churches.

2. On the peak of the Adam Hill in Ceylon, about 7,260 feet above the sea level, there is a four feet long print of human foot. Muslims believe that this is the footprint of Adam (a), the father of mankind. There is a *ḥadīth* to the effect that Adam first landed in India. The ancient India included Ceylon or Sri Lanka. But there are several different claims about this footprint. The Buddhists believe this to be that of the Buddha, Hindus to be that of Siva, and Christians to be that of St. Thomas. Therefore, it has become a place of importance to the followers of all these religions.

[Note by Nainar] The Adam's Peak in Ceylon is one of the loftiest and the best known in the world. It is 7,260 feet in height, rising in solitary grandeur on the western front of the great central plateau and could be seen by navigators miles away on the sea.

It is a great pilgrim centre to peoples of all nationalities. On its summit is a lofty black rock with a hollow depression about four feet long resembling a big human footprint. The Singhalese, Siamese, Burmese and Tibetans claim that it is the footprint of the Buddha and call it his *Sri pada*. The Hindus venerate it as the mark of Siva's foot. The Muslims consider it the footprint of Adam, who, according to them, having been sent out of paradise, stood on one foot on the peak for centuries doing penance. The Christians however claim it to be that of St. Thomas. The result is a never ending concourse of pilgrims to it from different countries.

There are two ways which lead to the peak. One is a straight narrow track along the precipices, the last portion of which is so steep that chains have been fixed at some places for the safety of pilgrims. The other is a circuitous road, considered less sacred.

Over the sacred footprint has been constructed a small chapel by the Buddhists to whom all offerings go, whether made by members of their own faith, of Hindus or Muslims. [Nainar]

3. The incident of the splitting of the moon was a miracle performed by the Prophet (s) taking the challenge of the non-believers in Makkah on 14 Dhū al-Ḥijjah, the fifth year before Hijrah. This incident is mentioned in Sūrah al-Qamar:1 in the Qur'an. Ibn Kathīr has included a great deal of credible description about this incident in his interpretation of the verse.

There is ample evidence to believe that the king named here had a vision of this miraculous incident and sought an explanation for it from his astrologers and was told that it was a miracle performed by a great man in Arabia.

4. There is a well-known tradition in Malabar contained in the *Keralolpatti*, a comparatively recent work of doubtful historical value, that the last Cheraman Perumal turned a Muslim in his old age, and went on a pilgrimage to Makkah after partitioning his kingdom among his friends, dependents and relatives. The early Muslim travellers who came to South India such as Sulaymān, the Venetian traveller Marco Polo, and later travellers like Ibn Baṭṭuṭah, and others do not make reference to this fact. It is said that there is a grave of a Malabar ruler at Zafar on the Arabian coast. If the report about a grave with an inscription can be relied upon, it may be the grave of one of the Zamorins who is said to have embraced Islam, perhaps as a result of a liaison which he seems to have had with a Moplah woman. This report gained currency only after the visit of 'Abd al-Razzāq to Calicut in 1442 and before the coming of the Portuguese to India in 1498.

Peoples of other religions also claim Cheraman Perumal as a convert to their respective faith. According to Faria Y. Souza, the Portuguese historian, Cheraman Perumal resolved to end his day at Meliapore (Mylapore in Madras) and went away to that place. Another account says that he went away to Bethlehem. Some say that he turned either a Buddhist or a Jain. It is known that one Bana, an ancestor of Cheraman Perumal became a convert to Buddhism. Perhaps this Bana is confounded with Cheraman Perumal. As for his conversion to Jainism there is no satisfactory evidence. But Hindu literary works of a canonical character like the *Periya Puranam, Tiruvilaiyadal Puranam* and *Halasya Mahatmyam* state that he was a devout Saiva throughout his life. It appears he continued to be a Hindu till the end of his life and died in the celebrated temple at Tiruvaneikkulam. [Nainar]

5. This is the famous king Cheraman Perumal. He is described in the history of Kerala with admiration as a king who was extremely concerned about the welfare of his subjects.

6. This is Pantalayani Kollam, a place near Koyilandi, Calicut. It was one of the famous ports of ancient Kerala. In the Arabic original it is called 'Fantarina'.

7. This was originally Darmapattanam, a place near Talassery, Kerala situated between two branches of Anjarakkandi River and Azhimukattu River. In the Arabic original it is called 'Dahfatan'.

8. Shahar al-Mukalla was an ancient city on the coast of Indian Ocean near Yemen. Today it is part of Salalah.

9. What one understands from here is that the king stayed a fairly long period at Shahar al-Mukalla on his way to Makkah to see the Prophet (s). But what one understands from the famous work *Malayalattile Mappilamar* is that he stopped there on his return from Makkah after visiting the Prophet (s). It is more likely to be true as the king had no chance of staying at Shahar al-Mukalla as he was eagerly going to meet the Prophet (s).

10. Why did the king instruct them to keep the news of his illness or demise a secret? Probably he thought only if they believed that he is alive and healthy, his words will be taken seriously and obeyed.

11. It was in 10 AH (632 AD) that Perumal died in Shahar al-Mukalla.

12. It was in Rajab, 21 AH that the aforementioned party of travellers arrived at Kodungallur. They postponed their journey on account of the sad demise of Perumal. This party under the leadership of Mālik bin Dīnār included twenty-two religious scholars as well.

13. This might be any of the kings of the Kochi dynasty.

14. The mosque they built at Kodungallur was the first Muslim mosque built in India. The materials required for its construction such as timber, bricks, etc., and the supervisors and expert workers were provided directly from the palace. The construction of this mosque, known as Cheraman Masjid, was finished on Monday, 11 Rajab, 21 AH according to *Malayalattile Mappilamar* by Rau Bahadur C. Gopalan Nair. It was Muḥammad bin Mālik who took charge as the *qāḍī* and *imām* of the mosque.

15 It was Mālik bin Ḥabīb who played the vital role in the propagation of Islam in Kerala. He travelled widely with a well-considered plan for this purpose.

16. Ezhimala is a hill range twenty-five kilometres north of Kannur on the sea front, 855 feet above the sea level. In the Arabic original it is called 'Haylī Marāwī'. William Logan has documented in the *Malabar Manual* that the

navigators of Vasco da Gama had told him about this hill range before setting out to Kerala. The construction of the Ezhimala mosque was finished on Thursday, 10 Dhū al-Ḥijjah, 21 AH and 'Abd al-Raḥmān bin Mālik was appointed *qāḍī* and *imām* there.

17. Today's Batkal is the Barkur of northern Karnataka. The word in the Arabic original is 'Fākkanūr'. The construction of the mosque here was completed on Thursday, 10 Rabī' al-Awwal, 22 AH. Ibrāhīm bin Mālik was appointed *qāḍī* and *imām* there.

18. This is the place called Mangalore, in Karnataka. In the Arabic text it is called 'Manjalūr'. They finished the construction of the mosque here on Friday, 27 Jamādī al-Awwal, 22 AH. Mūsā bin Mālik became the *qāḍī* and *imām* of this mosque.

19. This is Kasaragod, in the extreme north of Kerala. In the Arabic text the place is called 'Kānjrakūt'. The mosque construction here was over on Monday, 18 Rajab, 22 AH. The *qāḍī* appointed here was Mālik bin Muḥammad.

20. The word for Sreekandapuram in the Arabic text is 'Jurfatan'. There is a distance of about thirteen kilometres between Ezhimala and Sreekandapuram. It was on Thursday, 12 Sha'ban, 22 AH that they finished the construction of the mosque here. Shihāb al-Dīn 'Umar bin Muḥammad bin Mālik was appointed *qāḍī* here. The mosque at Darmadam was built on Thursday, 29 Sha'ban, 22 AH and the mosque at Pantalayani on Thursday, 21 Shawwāl, the same year. Ḥusayn bin Muḥammad bin Mālik became *qāḍī* at Darmadam and Zaynuddīn bin Mālik at Pantalayani. Chaliyam is near Beypore in modern Kozhikode district. In the Arabic text the word 'Shāliyāt' is used to refer to it. It is said that the mosque built here by Mālik bin Ḥabīb was the one known as Chaliyam Puzhakkara mosque. Zainuddin bin Muḥammad bin Mālik was the *qāḍī* of this mosque.

21. Khurasan is a province in the north east of Iran. Khurasan included a vast area in the past. Alexander's advent to India was through Khurasan.

22. The graves of both of them are in the southern side room of the Cheraman mosque in Kodungallur.

23. There are historians who find this quite likely. Rau Bahadur C. Gopalan Nair has documented this in detail in his *Malayalattile Mappilamar*. Accordingly, Perumal and the Prophet (s) met at Jeddah about nine in the morning on a Thursday, 27 Shawwāl. The Prophet (s) recited to him *kalimah al-tawḥīd* and he embraced Islam and took the name Tāj al-Dīn Sulṭān, stayed there for about five years and on his return died at Shahar al-Mukalla. Mr. Nair collected the information for this book from a historical document in Arabic in the possession of Rajamany Raja Sayid Ḥusayn bin Muḥammad bin 'Alī

Shihābuddīn Bā 'Alawī alias Mullah Koya Tangal, the big *qāḍī* of Calicut which the latter translated into Malayalam for him. This is quite vivid from the descriptions of the Arab historians. Mawlana Athar Mubarakpoori has quoted in his *Khilafate Rashida Aur Hindustan* an incident of some significance in this connection reported by the famous Ḥadīth scholar al-Ḥākim in his *al-Mustadrak*. Accordingly, "an Indian king gifted the Prophet (s) with a jar full of ginger and the Prophet took small pieces from it and gave them to his companions to eat." The king mentioned here is quite likely to be king Cheraman Perumal from Kerala. Arabs, those days, had better rapport with Kerala than with any other part of India, and Kerala was well-known for ginger cultivation. There are a number of other factors supportive of the above conclusion, for instance, the documents pertaining to the Arakkal royal family. The founder of this dynasty was Muḥammad 'Alī who was son of Perumal's sister Sreedevi. His original name was Mahabali. He embraced Islam and became Muḥammad 'Alī in 64 AH. The headquarters of this royal family was Darmadam. This means that Islam had arrived here and became dominant in this locality well before 200 AH.

The author's doubt on the probability of Perumal's meeting the Prophet (s) or embracing Islam during his time could be due to his notion concerning the period of Perumal's reign. But the view of some scholars is that the Perumal who met the Prophet (s) in person and embraced Islam was Palli Bana Perumal. In that case, the difference in chronology does not matter. Dr. Hermann Gundert's documentary history of Kerala *Keralolpatti* also talks about Perumal's embrace of Islam being during the time of the Prophet (s). According to *Tareekh-e-Ferishta*, a historical work by Muḥammad Qasim Ferishta, Perumal's embrace of Islam took place in the Prophet's 57th year. It is quite well known that the Prophet sent letters to the kings of various countries inviting them to Islam. Considering the trade relationship the Arabs of the time had with Malabar, the king of the place then was not likely to have been excluded from it.

24. Safar is situated near Sana'a, capital of Yemen. It is supposed that the grave in Safar bearing the name 'Abd al-Raḥmān Samuri might have been that of a king of the Zamorin dynasty who embraced Islam later on in the influence of the propagation of Mughīrah (r). That Perumal died and was buried at Shahar al-Mukalla is clearly stated by 'Umar bin Muḥammad Suhrawardī, a famous historian, Sufi, and the author of the famous work *Riḥlah al-Mulūk*.

25. Logan has published on the cover page of his *Malabar Manual* the picture of the sword Cheraman Perumal gave to the Zamorin advising: "You fight for it, killing and being killed."

26. *Tiruwadi* means the 'royal or sacred feet'. This had been the title of the Kings of the Venad (formerly Travancore) dynasty.

27. Edakkad is situated in Chelora Panchayat on the south of Kannur.

28. The Zamorin was supposed to have sworn, at the time of assuming power, to rule over the territory as a representative of Perumal who had left for Makkah. In certain places, the presence of the *qāḍī* and *imām* of the mosque was held essential for receiving the Zamorin.O

Section Three

1. The reference here might be to the suicide force—*chavettu pada*—of Kerala of that age. The motto of this force was: "kill or be killed". There are references to this force in Kaudilya's *Artasastra*. This is also called "garudasambradayam". The choric song "chaverpadapat" is quite well-known. Even today, there are suicide squads for many goals in several parts of the world.

2. This situation has changed a great deal today among the Muslims following better awareness about the religious teachings.

3. Dr. C. Achyuta Menon, Head of the Malayalam Department, University of Madras, has kindly furnished the following note on Nair marriage:
The marriage customs of Malabar are very often misunderstood, particularly the system that once obtained among the Nairs.
There seems to be a general impression that the relationship between men and women among the Nairs was rather loose and the practice of polyandry was usually associated with them. We get varying descriptions of them from the accounts of travellers who often generalise from a few stray cases that come to their notice without any reference to the social setting or background. Sometimes the travellers come into contact with the lower strata of the society, and form impressions from their habits.
The question was thoroughly examined by the Malabar marriage commission in 1894, and in the dissenting minute written in that connection, one of its members the late O. Candu Menon, the leading jurist and novelist of the time, has established on unimpeachable evidence that polyandry was never a general practice among the Nairs, although it was possible to point out isolated instances among them, probably copied from the artisan classes among whom it was the general custom. A Nair marriage has all the validity of a sacred rite as understood and practiced among other communities in Malabar and outside. It is always performed in public before respectable persons of the locality. The birth and death ceremonies of the Nair community emphatically support this view. In the former the father has a definite function to perform, and in the latter the son of the deceased takes his place along with his nephews. Probably the system of inheritance namely, Marumakkattayam, by which the nephews inherit the properties of the uncles whose sons have no legal right to their father's properties, is responsible for the confused thinking on the subject. Inheritance is a matter of economic arrangement and the comparative merits of the Matriarchal and Patriarchal systems of inheritance are a matter of opinion.

There is one peculiarity about the Nair marriage, that is, both the parties to the marriage have a right to divorce if they wished to do so. This does not, however, mean that the conjugal bond between them is not of a fixed character. The institution of marriage has an interesting history in Malabar and the changes that threw the original *tali-kettu* (*tali*-tying) ceremony to the background and brought into being a simple ceremony called Pudavamuri (cloth-cutting), dropping all ritualistic details of the former, deserves closer study in its proper perspective. See also the remarks given by F. Fawcett, in *Madras Government Museum Bulletin*, Vol. III, No. 3, pp. 228-229. [Nainar]

4. This is the old practice of *talikettukalyanam*. It is not prevalent today.

5. This type of marriages, known as "pandawacharam", is no longer practised today. According to certain reports, such families were seen until 1963 or so.

6. Perhaps the author refers to the Nambootiri women who do not appear before men except close relatives, like brothers and junior brothers-in-law. But the Nambootiri women go out to temples and attend social functions in their own community accompanied by Nair women. On such occasions the Nambootiri women wrap themselves up except their faces with a long sheet of white cloth (*kacca*) about eighteen cubits long. They hold an umbrella (*marakkuta*) to hide their face with it, and they never part with it till they return home. The word *marakkuta* consists of two parts, *mara* (to hide), *kuta* (an umbrella); the compound meaning, an umbrella to hide oneself. [Nainar]

7. The womenfolk of the Nambootiri families were known as 'Antarjanangal', and in the interior country side they were called 'Aattol'. They were called so because they remained mostly indoors.

8. The mention of various ranks among the Brahmans is probably based on their distinctive traits. The Brahmans of Malabar may be classified under four broad divisions, namely Nambootiris, Tulu Brahmans, Tamil Brahmans or Bhattars and Sarasvat Brahmans or Konkanis. The first constitute a dignified and cultured class. They are kept above want and they minister to the spiritual and temporal wants of the people. The Tulu Brahmans who were immigrants from the Tulu country or South Canara and still continue to be largely temple priests. The Tamil Brahmans were immigrants to Malabar from the Cola and Pandya countries in search of fortune. The Konkani Brahmans are largely traders in Malabar and have their own temples for worship. [Nainar]

9. The various ranks among the Nairs are:
Aristocracy: The class from which ruling families were drawn. Most of the royal families in Malabar today are the representatives of this class.
Feudatory chieftains: This class comes next to the aristocracy. They assume different titles as Kaimal, Nair, Panikkar, Menon, Nambiar, Kurup, etc.

Kiriattil Nair or *Illakkar*: They are the intermediary class. They have no social status now. They are employed generally as cooks by the high class Nairs on occasions of Sraddha ceremonies.

Lower classes: There are a large number of lower classes of Nairs called Sudra Nair, Vattekkatt Nair, Attikkurussi, Anturan, following certain professions, like oil-monger, etc. They are also employed by people of higher castes during the period when pollution is observed. Some of these classes are considered untouchables in certain parts of Malabar.

Ambalavasis or *temple servants*: It is supposed by some people that these are outcastes from the fold of high class Nairs. They are divided into a number of sects and sub-sects with varying status which they acquired by their contact with Nambootiris.

At the present day the term Nair is applied in a general sense to a number of classes with different status, some of which are indicated above.

For details, See F. Fawcett, *Madras Government Museum Bulletin*, Vol. III, No. 3, pp. 185-224. [Nainar]

10. These customs are known as "mannappedi", "pulappedi", etc. Historians differ as to the origin of these customs. The Pulaya people used to suffer great deal of persecution for this especially during the Karkidaka month. This custom was abolished in Travancore in 1696 AD by Umayamma Rani at the direction of her advisor Kottayam Kerala Warma.

11. This practice prevalent among the Nambootiris was known as "sambantam". This continued until the early years of the twentieth century when there arose large-scale protests against this from within the Nair and Nambootiri communities.

Section Four

Chapter One

1. The Portuguese navigator Vasco da Gama and his band of people landed at Kappad, in Chemanchery Panchayat, in Koyilandi Taluk, fifteen kilometres north of Calicut. This was on 17 May, 1498. Another opinion is that it was on the 11th and 20th of the same month. St. Raphael, St. Gabriel, and St. Michael were the three ships by which they arrived. There is a monument commemorative of his arrival on Kappad beach.

2. Mas'ūdī, who quotes from *al-Mudkhal al-Kabīr ilā 'Ilm al-Nujūm* (Great Introduction to Astronomy) by Abū Ma'shar al-Balkhī has given an account of the Indian season. He says that the stormy and quiet seasons in the eastern seas begin when the sun is in the signs of the zodiac and that it is impossible to sail from Oman on the sea of Hind in the Tirmah (June) except with first-rate vessels and light cargoes. These vessels are called al-Tirmahiyyah. In Hind at that time is winter and the rainy season; for the two Syriac months called

Kanun and the month Shobat (December, January and February) are their summer months. Our winter is their summer, while the month Tamus (July) and Ab (August) which are summer months with us, are their winter. This change of seasons is the case in all the towns of Hind, Sind and the neighbouring countries, through the whole extent of these seas. [Nainar]

3. The ruler of Calicut, the Zamorin, volunteered to receive Vasco da Gama and his people respectfully. But he sent them back saying that he shall consider the idea of having trade relations with Portugal later. This disappointed Gama. That the merchandises he had brought could not be disposed of here added to his sadness. He concluded that it was the Muslims in the locality that persuaded the Zamorin to take an unfavourable attitude to him and thus thwarted his plans. Disrupting the Malabar Muslims' trade with Arabia was one of his plans. Thus this time they returned home to come prepared to realise this goal. They left Calicut on 29 August, 1498 and went ashore to Kannur and made a rapport with Kolattiri, returning to Portugal on 20 November of the same year.

4. The Portuguese group referred to here is the one that arrived at Calicut on 13 September 1500, under the leadership of General Pedro Alvaris Cabral. Although there were 33 ships and 1,500 people in his party when he set out, only six ships reached Malabar. (It is said that the agricultural produces like cashew nut, pineapple, pears, etc., were introduced in Kerala by them. It has been observed that the sexually transmitted disease syphilis, called "parankippunnu"—a disease named after the Portuguese in Malayalam—also was spread here by them. Although Cabral and the Zamorin had discussions on 18 September, they could not reach any consensus. Many discussions followed between their representatives, and eventually they got permission to build a factory in Calicut. But they were forced to move to Kochi before long because of their arrogance, their atrocities on Muslims and their claims on the sea. On 24 December 1500, Cabral and his people arrived at Kochi. Unnigodawarma Tirumulpad, the king of Kochi, who was in enmity with Calicut then, received Cabral and his people and gave them permission to build a fort there. The fort thus built was the Manual fort, its foundation stone was laid on 26 September 1503.

5. Cabral actually had fled to Kannur in fear at the sight of the Zamorin's naval forces coming towards Kochi. He made a treaty with Kolattiri, the ruler of Kolattunad, the territory between the south of modern Kannur city and the Neeleswaram river. When, eventually, he returned home, he had only five ships to take with him out of the 33 that he had come with. It is said that he was not assigned any responsibility afterwards.

6. The reference here might be to the military expedition led by the naval captain Joao de Nova.

7. This was the second coming of Vasco da Gama. The Portuguese king had appointed him as the admiral of the naval expeditions to India, Persia and

Arabia. There were seven military heads also with him. Gama and his forces set out, this time, on 10 February 1502, in 15 ships. Later on, Stephen da Gama joined them with five ships. They arrived at the coast of Malabar, killing many and looting many others on the way. His actions were that of "a devil in the shape of a man", according to Logan, author of the *Malabar Manual*. He was the admiral who, after attacking a ship with 400 pilgrims including women and children returning to Malabar after the pilgrimage to Makkah, ordered to set fire on it with all of them aboard. This was but one of the many cruelties of Gama. Arriving at Calicut via Kannur, he asked the Zamorin to evict the Muslims from the city. As the Zamorin did not oblige, he attacked the city. He further plundered the 24 ships which had arrived at Calicut laden with rice and threw overboard the 800 mariners on it after chopping off their limbs. Another of Gama's monstrous actions was how he dealt with the Zamorin's messenger Talappanna Nambootiri. Gama chopped off his arms, nose and ears and festooned him with it and sent him to the Zamorin with a note asking to cook it for eating. The Zamorin took an oath to fight the Portuguese at any cost. It was thus the naval force of Khawājah Qāsim set out at sea. Sensing this, Gama withdrew to Kochi, and had a treaty with Unnirama Warma, the king of Kochi, and left for Portugal with his ships laden with pepper, cardamom and other produces, leaving behind in Kochi about 200 Portuguese to meet the forces of the Zamorin coming to attack Kochi. Thus, he escaped meeting the forces led by Khawājah Amber and Khawājah Qāsim. On March 15, 1503, the Zamorin, coming via Edappally, attacked Kochi. The Kochi king Unnirama Warma, who was defeated in the confrontation, sought refuge in a temple together with his Portuguese soldiers.

8. This time the commander of the Portuguese forces was Colonel Durate Pacheco. It was this Portuguese colonel who liberated Kochi from the Zamorin. He was the officer in charge of the Portuguese fort in Kochi. After the battle with the Zamorin, Pachico set fire on the houses (*illam*) of the Nambootiris near Kochi and confiscated their lands and gave them to the Christians.

9. Mahmud Shah I was the sultan who ruled over Gujarat between 1458 and 1511 AD. The Adil Shah mentioned here was Ismail Adil Shah, the governor of Bijapur between 1510 and 1534 AD under the Adil Shahi reign.

10. Sultan Qānṣūh al-Ghawrī was the last king of the slave dynasty of Egypt. The period of his reign was from 1510 to 1516 AD. The slave dynasty ended with the death of Qānṣūh al-Ghawrī in a struggle with Salīm Shāh I, the ruler of the Ottoman Constantinople.

11. This is an island, south of Gujarat.

12. This is *qāḍī* Malik Iyās, who ruled over Diu under the Gujarat ruler Muhammad Begaro.

13. Of the Portuguese forces who fought under Lorenzo de Almeida, son of the Portuguese viceroy, 140 were killed and as many were injured. The Portuguese

forces had to admit defeat before the clever and strategic cannon attack of Amīr Ḥusayn. Lorenzo was killed in this struggle.

14. This battle that took place on 3 February 1509 was led by the Portuguese Viceroy Almeida himself. The sudden withdrawal of Mālik Iyās is blamed for the victory of the Portuguese. Malik Iyās, a Russian who had embraced Islam, was the governor of Diu under the Gujarat sultan. It is said that Almeida had won him to his side by bribing. This victory, however, enabled the Portuguese to establish their domination over the Arabian Ocean.

15. Camran is an island in the Red Sea close to southern Yemen.

16. Sharīf Barakāt was the ruler of Ḥijāz from 1504 AD. Once, the Turks took him to Egypt as a captive. Back in Ḥijāz sometime later, Barakāt continued to be its ruler until his death.

17. Sultan Salīm Shāh was the Sultan of Turkey who put an end to the Mamlūk dynasty by killing Qānṣūh al-Ghawrī in 1516 AD and ruled over Egypt till 1519 AD. After his death he was succeeded by Sulaymān the Magnificent (1520-1566). See Sir William Muir, *The Mameluke or Slave Dynasty of Egypt*, pp. 196-214. [Nainar]

18. This happened in the leadership of Alfonso de Albuquerque in January, 1510 AD. He was the Portuguese viceroy of the territory from Gujarat to Kanyakumari. The territories between the Cape of Good Hope and Gujarat were in the control of George de Aguiar and the territories east of Kanyakumari were under Diago Lopez de Sequira. Although Albuquerque took charge as viceroy only on 8 March 1509, he had visited Kochi in 1503 under General Cabral and later in 1506. He had an irresoluble hatred towards Islam and the Arabs and was looking for an opportunity to bring about their destruction. He was extremely cruel and vicious in nature and at the same time very intelligent and cunning.

19. The Persian word *naquda* means captain of a ship. The Mithqal mosque in Kuttichira, Calicut, is the reconstructed form of the mosque built originally by an Arab named Naquda Mithqal.

20. This confrontation that began on 4 January 1510 was spearheaded by Manual Fernando de Continho. Albuquerque's plan was to propitiate the Zamorin in a diplomatic way. But Cutinho insisted on having a confrontation. He had arrived from Portugal with the Portuguese king's instruction to burn Calicut. While the Zamorin was away in Chettuwa for another battle, they took opportunity and together with their soldiers besieged the fort. But the brave resistance of the Nair soldiers using arrows and spears humbled them and they had to flee for life abjectly defeated. Cutinho was killed and Albuquerque seriously injured in the struggle. Albuquerque could escape from the scene only narrowly and that too under the cover of Portuguese fire from the sea. Koyappakki, who had earlier helped Gama market his merchandise in Calicut,

had approached the Portuguese asking to avoid this confrontation. But the Portuguese instead put him in prison and did not heed to his words. This provoked Koyappakki greatly and turned him against to the Portuguese ever since.

21. Situated on the south of the Arabian peninsula, Aden is a major port on the Red Sea and the economic capital of Yemen. Albuquerque had left Malabar for Goa in September 1512, and it was from there that he set out to Aden. As his campaign against Aden ended up in failure, he returned to Kochi in August 1513.

22. This is Amīr Marjān al-ʿĀmirī.

23. Earlier the queen of Kollam had invited Vasco da Gama to establish warehouses and commercial centres in her country. It was the queen who paved the way for the Portuguese to plunder Kollam and ceaselessly continue there with their plots against the Muslims.

24. Situated on the western coast of India between Maharashtra and Karnataka, Goa is today one of the states of India, with Panaji as its capital.

25. Goa belonged to Vijayanagar. A few years before 1507 AD it was captured by Yusuf Adil Shah of Bijapur. The king of Vijayanagar appointed one Timoja as the commandant of the Vijayanagar fleet on the west coast in order to wage war and recapture Goa. After the death of Yusuf Adil Shah in 1510 AD, Alfonso de Albuquerque, the then Viceroy of the Portuguese possessions in the East, was persuaded by Timoja to attack Goa, taking advantage of the young age of Ismail Adil Shah of Bijapur who had just then succeeded his father. The Portuguese took possession of Goa in March 1510. Ismail Adil Shah took it back two months later. But in November of the same year the Portuguese recaptured it and made it their capital. Being centrally situated on the west coast, it enjoyed a commanding position for commercial purposes. (Rev. H. Heras, *Aravidu Dynasty*, Vol. I, p. 57; M. S. Commissariat, *History of Gujarat*, p.252). [Nainar]

26. It was on 3 October 1510 that Albuquerque set out from Kannur to attack Goa. He occupied Goa while Adil Khan was away. However, Ismail Adil Shah, the sultan of Bijapur, recaptured Goa from him in two months. Before long, the Portuguese recaptured it again. In 1535, they also captured Diu. Since then Goa remained a Portuguese colony until its independence was declared on 19 December 1961 and thereby it became part of Indian Union.

Chapter Two

1. The attitude of the Portuguese to the Muslims was one of inveterate hostility on account of rivalry in trade. Since the days of John III of Portugal (1521-57 AD) proslytism became one of the objects of the Portuguese policy in India.

They also committed many excesses. In 1560 they established the inquisition at Goa. They did not scruple to destroy mosques for the construction of churches. (See *Tuḥfāt-al-Mujāhidīn* translated into English by Lieut. M. J. Rowlandson, pp. 103-105 fn.) [Nainar]

2. Konkan is a coastal plain near the Western Ghats stretching from Daman on the north to Goa on the south.

Chapter Three

1. The struggle that began against Cabral in 1500 AD lasted for about 14 or 15 years by then. The Portuguese were the biggest superpower of the world with the most modern weapons then. And the Muslims were weak and without any of the sophisticated weapons.

2. Although Albuquerque tried his best to establish rapport with the Zamorin, his efforts yielded no result. The Zamorin was fully aware of the treacherous ways of the Portuguese and the consequences of their establishing roots here. Eventually, the Elankoor Nambiatiri Tirumulpad of Ernad poisoned the Zamorin to death at the behest of Albuquerque. Thus he became the new Zamorin. Albuquerque made a treaty with the new Zamorin. The terms and conditions of this treaty signed at Kannur on 24 December 1513 were quite favourable to the Portuguese. It was Don Garcia de Noronha, Albuquerque's representative, who negotiated the terms on the Portuguese side.

3. The fort was built on the northern bank of the Kallayi River, on the southern border of Calicut city. Thomas Fernandez was in charge of the mission.

4. The author is not quite correct. There were a number of disputes and quarrels among the Portuguese who came here. When Albuquerque was appointed as viceroy to replace Almeida, the latter did not accept him, instead he put him in prison on his arrival here. Eventually, Almeida volunteered to quit only after the arrival of Cutinho and the Kochi king's notice to him that he would only deal with Albuquerque as Portuguese viceroy. Almeida was killed in a fight while looting an African village on his way to Europe after he lost his power as viceroy. Likewise, the author may not be aware of the feuds between Mascaranus and Lopo Vaz da Sampayov, and Lopo Vaz da Sampayov and Nuno da Aqcuina. Yet compared with the disunity among the Muslim Emirs and leaders, these were quite insignificant. In spite of all the feuds and disunities, they were all united against the Muslims. And that is the spirit of the statement here.

5. This secret attempt on the Zamorin took place in 1517 AD. This murder attempt was said to be on the instigation of the Kochi king who was very unhappy over the treaty the Portuguese had with the Zamorin. He wanted to sow the seeds of discord between them. Albuquerque was not alive when the incident took place. He had died in 1515 AD following a cardiac arrest. The

Portuguese viceroy after him was Lopo Zoirus. [This incident is referred to only in this work. Note by Husain Nainar to his translation, Madras, 1942]

Chapter Four

1. This is Kakkad in Kannur district. In the Arabic original it is 'Kabkad'.

2. This is Tikkodi in Kozhikode district. In the Arabic original it is 'Tirkudi'.

3. This is Parappanangadi in Malappuram district. In the Arabic original it is 'Parpurangadi'.

4. This is Tirurangadi in Malappuram district. In the Arabic original it is 'Tiruwarangad'.

5. This is Tanur in Malappuram district. In the Arabic original, it is the same.

6. This is Parawanna near Tirur in Malappuram district. In the Arabic original it is 'Parawannur'.

7. Ponnani in Malappuram district is a very old port. This is where the Bharata River (Bharatappuzha) joins the Arabian ocean. This city had very ancient ties with the Arabs. In the Arabic original it is 'Fonnan'.

8. This is the Weliancode region in Ponnani Taluk in Malappuram district. 'Umar Qāḍī, the great scholar, poet and an uncompromising anti-imperialist, was buried here. In the Arabic original it is 'Baliankut'.

9. Kannur is a city of antiquity of the Northern Malabar. The ancient travellers like Pliny and Ptolemy have mentioned this city in their works. In the Arabic original it is 'Kannanur'.

10. This is Tiruwangad in the Talassery Municipality of Kannur district.

11. This might be Chemnad in Kasaragod Taluk in Kasaragod district. Chemnad is a *panchayat*. In the Arabic original it is 'Chemmanaya'.

12. The Marakkar family was well established in trade and commerce at the time of the arrival of the Portuguese in Kerala. Some people believe that they are descendants of the ancient Arab settlers of this place. But the majority believes them to be genuine Mappilas in view of the characteristics of Malayalam language in their names. However, they came to be known as great fighters only after their migration from Kochi to Calicut and Ponnani. Afterwards, the Marakkars, who were the leaders of the Zamorin's naval forces, became the dreaded nightmares for the Portuguese all over Asia. Their arrival made a turning point in the Malabar people's resistance to the invading Portuguese. The western historians, however, represent them as pirates, out of grudge and malice.

13. This war was spearheaded on the Portuguese side by Don Henrique de Menezes. After Albuquerque, Lopo Zoirus and Diago Lopus Sequira were the Portuguese viceroys here before Don Henrik Menezes. All of them were notorious for their cruelties and atrocities. Menezes arrived in Calicut as the Portuguese viceroy in January 1523. His goal was, reportedly, maintaining peace in Malabar and propagating Christianity there. However, as he arrived in Malabar he became more cruel than his predecessors. In the battle of Ponnani, the Portuguese had the support of Purakkat Arayan, the leader of the naval forces of Chempakassery Rajah (Ambalappuzha dynasty). As the battle was in progress, Menezes justifiably suspected that Arayan was more interested in looting and plundering than waging battle. Therefore, he gave orders to kill him. However, Arayan escaped, although seriously wounded.

It was at this juncture that Gama once again arrived in Malabar. This time he came as the Portuguese viceroy. This was in September 1524, twenty years after his previous visit. However, he could not do much this time as he died on 24 December, 1524. He was buried in the cemetery of St. Antony's Church in Fort Kochi. For the Zamorin and the Muslims of Malabar, it was a period of unprecedented glory and empowerment on account of the wonderful war skills of Kunhali I (Kuttiali).

14. The Portuguese forces had organized themselves for war in Calicut under the leadership of Captain Don Jawo de Lima. On the side of the Zamorin, besides Tenancheri Ilayatu, Kurumbranat Rajah also brought his forces to Calicut to fight against the Portuguese. The Muslims were led in the battle by a European engineer who had abandoned Christianity and embraced Islam, as Logan points out in the *Malabar Manual*. However, there is no doubt about the fact that it was the clever and strategic movements of Kuttiali that forced the Portuguese to abandon the fort and flee for life. The Zamorin had not personally joined this battle with his forces until 15 June 1525.

15. This attack on the Muslim ships was under the leadership of the Portuguese viceroy Henrik Menezes. In the meanwhile, Menezes sustained a serious injury on his leg in a confrontation with the small conventional boats near Beypore. Another confrontation near Mahe worsened his condition and eventually he died on 2 February 1526 at Kannur and was buried there. Following that, Lopo Vaz da Sampayo became the new viceroy.

16. At this stage the Portuguese viceroy in India was General Lopo Vaz da Sampayo. It was in October 1529 that Nuno da Aquino became the new viceroy removing him from that position.

17. Ponnani was a strategically important place. This port had very good trade relations with the Arabs and it was this port the Marakkars, who set out from Kochi to fight the Portuguese, first took for their headquarters. It was following the Portuguese invasion of Ponnani in 1524 AD that the Marakkars moved to Putuppattanam and made it their new operational base.

18. Surat is the name of a district as well as a district headquarters in Gujarat. It lies between Cam Bay sea on the west and the Eastern Ghats on the east. It is 260 kilometres north of Mumbai. Jujar might be 'Janjira', a port on the south of Mumbai.

Chapter Five

1. This shrewd and scheming Portuguese leader might be Diago de Sylveira. Logan has made clear in the *Malabar Manual* that the Zamorin in power then was eager to have a treaty with the Portuguese ever since the arrival of Nuno da Aquina as their viceroy. Chaliyam was a strategically important place. The Portuguese were aware of its importance in trade and military movements. If they could build a fort there, they would also be able to understand the trends in the trade between Arabia and Calicut very well. They could somehow manage to bring the Zamorin round to permit them to build a fort there. The Tanur king also played a big role in it. It was only after four decades that the ruler of Calicut could bring the fort under his control.

2. This was Chaliyam Puzhakkara mosque, one of the seven mosques built by Mālik bin Dīnār in Kerala.

3. It was Nuno da Aquina, the Portuguese viceroy, who responded so after hearing the complaints of the Muslims. What Logan has stated in the *Malabar Manual* is that the mosque and the premises were sold to the Portuguese by the Muslim *mu'adhdhin* in charge of the mosque and that the Zamorin took disciplinary action against him for it. The word the author used in the Arabic original is *rai'* which means 'the ruler'. The same is the word used to refer to the Zamorin and the other kings in the book. That is why the word 'king' is used here to suggest it.

4. It has been made clear in Section Two that if ever the Zamorin had any confrontation with a weaker king in Malabar, it would end up in a treaty, by which, as per conventions, the defeated king would give the Zamorin enough wealth or the country as a whole in compensation.

5. Amīr Muṣṭafā bin Bahrām al-Rūmī was the military chief of the Gujarat ruler Bahadur Shah. He was also known as Rumi Khan and Khawajah. He betrayed Bahadur Shah and that facilitated the Mughal King Humayun to take over Gujarat.

[Note by Nainar] Amīr Muṣṭafā, son of Bahrām of Constantinople was the nephew of Salmān Ra'īs, a Turk admiral and adventurer who entered the service of Salīm Shāh of Rūm and eventually became the lord of Yemen. On the death of his uncle in 1529 AD Amīr Muṣṭafā became the master of the Abyssinian slaves. His father Bahrām gave orders that he shculd help Bahadur Shah of Gujarat against the Portuguese. Amīr Muṣṭafā arrived at Diu in 1531 AD and was received by Malik Tughan, son of Malik Iyās, the governor of the place. Amīr Muṣṭafā fought against the Portuguese and defeated them in a naval engagement off Diu in 1531 AD Bahadur Shah, the Sultan of Gujarat conferred upon Amīr Muṣṭafā the title of Rumi Khan in recognition of his services and gave him as his fiefs Rander, Surat and all the adjoining coast as far as Mahim. Later Bahadur Shah made him the Governor of Diu dismissing Malik Tughan from that office. But Amīr Muṣṭafā deserted Bahadur Shah in 1535 AD and took service under the Mughal emperor Humayun when he invaded Gujarat. Amir Muṣṭafā died at Chunar in 1538 AD. See M. S. Commissariat, *History of Gujarat*, pp. 338-39. [Nainar]

6. Mocha is a port city in Yemen. Its importance declined as Aden rose into prominence as a centre of trade and commerce.

Chapter Six

1. The Portuguese leader mentioned here is their viceroy Nuno da Aquina.

2. Bahadur Shah made this request to the Zamorin as he was quite sure that only people of Malabar, especially the Marakkars, were capable of defeating the Portuguese in a sea battle. However, the Zamorin did not entertain this, probably because they have already signed the treaty.

Chapter Seven

1. Humayun was son of Zahiruddin Muhammad Babar (1483–1530 AD), the founder of the Mughal dynasty in India. Born in Kabul, Humayun was a powerful ruler of the Mughal dynasty. Reputed as a poet and a great scholar of Persian and Turkish, Humayun inherited kingship at the death of his father.

2. Mahim is a place north of Mumbai city. Vasai is further north of Mahim.

3. Bahadur Shah regretted his own action afterwards and began to think about the ways of retrieving the territories he had lost. Sensing this, the Portuguese viceroy Nuno invited the Sultan to Diu and arranged to treacherously murder him as he was returning after the discussions. As planned, the Portuguese murdered the Sultan and threw his body overboard into the sea.

[Note by Nainar] Bahadur Shah ceded the island of Diu in 1535 AD to the Portuguese for their help against Humayun Badshah, and permitted them to erect a fort in that island. But subsequently he regretted his act and wanted to drive the Portuguese out of Diu. The Portuguese viceroy Nuno da Kunha was also aware of the Sultan's ideas. In 1537 while Bahadur Shah was returning after a visit to the viceroy at Diu, he met his tragic end. The evidences regarding his sudden death are conflicting. According to some he was drowned; some say he was killed. But it appears the Portuguese were responsible for his death. See M. S. Commissariat, *History of Gujarat*, pp. 374-383. [Nainar]

4. Kutty Ibrahim Marakkar was the nephew of Ali Ibrahim Marakkar.

5. Kayal Pattanam is a reputed place situated on the bank of the Tamraparni River in Tirunelveli, Tamilnadu. The place was legendarily known for the arrival of Marco Polo, and also for the famous Sufi Shaykh 'Abd al-Qādir. Kayal Pattanam is also known for a dispute between the Parawas and the Muslims over fishing rights. The Portuguese joined the Parawa side in the dispute and the Parawas, in gratitude, volunteered to embrace Christianity. It was in this connection that Ali Ibrahim Marakkar went to Kayal Pattanam to help the Muslims against the Portuguese.

6. This is Beetala in the text in Arabic original. It is on the south of Kayal Pattanam.

7. This is Nalleppilly, a locality in the old Kochi state. Ali Ibrahim Marakkar was mortally wounded in the confrontation and breathed his last in a mosque on his return.

Chapter Eight

1. Sulaymān Bāshā was one of the generals of Sultan Salīm of Rūm. He accompanied Sultan Salīm in his expedition for the conquest of Egypt in 1516 AD. In 1525 he was made the governor of that province by Sultan Sulaymān the Magnificent. In 1535 he was sent to Yemen and Aden to put down a rebellion. On his return in 1537 he was again made governor of Egypt. On the death of Bahadur Shah of Gujarat in 1537, Sultan Sulaymān the Magnificent ordered Sulaymān Bāshā to proceed to Diu with a large fleet to put an end to the power of the Portuguese in India. Sulaymān Bāshā started for India in June 1537 and on his way sacked Aden early in August and hanged the Arab ruler of the place Shaykh 'Āmir bin Dāwūd along with other leading nobles. See M. S. Commissariat, *History of Gujarat*, pp. 400-402.

2. It was at the time when the Portuguese military head Martin de Souza had gathered all their strength and pledged to destroy the military power of the Muslims; Sulaymān Bāshā was brought to the forefront by the Turkish viceroy in Egypt. He did so at the request of the Zamorin.

3. 'Āmir bin Dāwūd was the last Sultan of the Banā Ṭāhir dynasty that ruled over Yemen. He was a young and generous ruler who was deeply concerned about the welfare of the people. Quite naturally everybody loved him dearly. Therefore, everybody felt angry with Sulaymān Bāshā for killing him. It is said that Sulaymān Bāshā was persuaded to kill him because of his impression that 'Āmir had befriended the Portuguese secretly.

4. Why did Sulaymān Bāshā return without waging a war although he had come fully prepared for it? There are those of the opinion that it was because the Portuguese had fled the scene, scared by the performance of the Egyptian

forces. But, in fact, the real reason was that the people of this country hated him and did not cooperate with him in the war on account of his cruel murder of the innocent 'Āmir bin Dāwūd and the looting of Aden. Whatever was the reason, Sulaymān Bāshā's return was a big blow to the Zamorin, and to Kerala and India as a whole. The magnitude of its consequences was even to the extent of the Zamorin being forced to have compromise with the Portuguese.

5. This party set out to Ceylon following the request of the traders in Ceylon to the Zamorin to help them resist the Portuguese. There are differences as to how Kunhali Marakkar was killed. Some believe that he was a victim of megalomania. Some others think that he was one of those who were treacherously killed by Mayadunne, brother of the king of Ceylon.

Chapter Nine

1. This treaty was signed on 12 January 1540. Persuaded and pressured by the kings of Tanur and Kodungallur, the Zamorin, in his abject condition, promised to the Portuguese that he will not set out any war ship or boats with armed men at sea and further that he will not have any trade with the Arabs. The Portuguese viceroy then was Gartia da Norana, the successor of Nuno da Aquino. This treaty was a great deal of shame and humiliation to the Zamorin and posed great danger to the Muslims. Henceforth Muslims could not engage in any trade without the permission of the Portuguese. Kunhali II challenged the Portuguese by intensifying his guerrilla warfare against them.

2. He appears to have been the chief of Cannanore about 1545 AD. The history of the family of Ali Adhiraja is shrouded in mystery. According to *Keralolpathi*, Cheraman Perumal invited a Muslim family from a place called Aryapuram and installed it at Cannanore. But according to local tradition the earliest ancestor of the family of Adhiraja was a Nair called Arayan Kulangara Nair, one of the ministers of Kolattiri (Chirakkal Raja). This Nair is said to have lived about the beginning of the twelfth century AD. It is believed he became a convert to Islam and took the name Muhammad or Muhammad Ali. He continued to be minister of Kolattiri. After his death his descendants ruled over Cannanore with the title 'Ali Raja'.

3. Abu Bakar Ali was nephew of the famous Mammali Marakkar.

Chapter Ten

1. This might be the king of Wadakkumkur. The territories in the dominion of this dynasty were Ettumanur, Waikom, Meenachal, Todupuzha, and Muwattupuzha.

2. Logan's *Malabar Manual* makes it clear that about a third of those who lived in Pantalayani Kollam were martyred.

3. Keelakkara is in Tamilnadu. In the Arabic original it is 'Kirakara'.

4. The people of 'Ād, and their prophet Hūd, are mentioned in the Qur'an in many places. They occupied a large tract of country in southern Arabia, extending from Oman at the mouth of the Persian Gulf to Hadhramawt and Yemen at the southern end of the Red Sea. The people were tall in stature and were great builders. They forsook God, and oppressed their people. A three-year famine visited them, but they took no heed. At length a terrible blast of wind destroyed them and their land.

[Note by Nainar] The Thamūd people were the successors to the culture and civilisation of the 'Ād. They were cousins to the 'Ād, apparently a younger branch of the same race. Their seat was in the north-west corner of Arabia (Arabia Petraea) between Madīnah and Syria. With the advance of material civilization, the Thamūd people became godless and arrogant. Their prophet and warner was Ṣāliḥ. They did not pay any heed to his warnings. When the cup of their iniquities was full, the Thamūd people were destroyed by a dreadful earthquake, which threw them prone on the ground and buried them with their houses. See Sūrah al-A'rāf: 65-79. [Nainar]

5. Maldives is an archipelago consisting of over 2000 little islands situated on the south of India and southwest of Sri Lanka. It is a much favoured tourist centre today. Its language is Mahel. It was with the help of this Turk Yūsuf that the Zamorin's forces could capture Punnakkayal which had been in the dominion of Manual Rodrigo.

6. These cannons were very helpful for the Zamorin in his attack on the Portuguese.

Chapter Eleven

1. What provoked the dispute was that the Muslims challenged the condition in the treaty between the Portuguese and the Zamorin that the latter's subjects shall have any trade trips only with a license from the Portuguese.

2. The 'Lakshadweep' in the Arabian Ocean might be referred to here. The northern islands of this group had been under the rule of Arakkal Ali Raja until 1787 AD. It was on November 1 1973 that these islands were officially called Lakshadweep.

3. Of the 36 small islands of the Lakshadweep only 10 are inhabited. These are about 260 to 440 kilometres from Kochi. The author has mentioned only nine islands. In the Arabic original their names are: Ammīnī, Kardīb, Andrūt, Kalfīnī, Miluki, Agatti, Kanjamanhal, Kaltan and Sheetilakam.

4. Āshī is likely to be north of Sumatra. Danāṣarī might be Danao of Philippines.

5. Honnawaram is in the northern Canara district of Karnataka. In the Arabic original it is 'Hannūr'.

6. Aceh (in the Arabic text 'Al-Āshī') is on the northern tip of Sumatra Island. The first Muslim emperor of Aceh was 'Alī Mughāyit Shāh alias al-Kāmil. Islam reached here through Arab and Indian traders.

7. It is said that it was an everyday hobby for the Portuguese mariner Dementesov to behead people and throw them overboard wrapped in mats.

Chapter Twelve

1. Kuttipocker was better known as Kunhali Marakkar II.

[Note by Nainar] Kutti, in Malayalam and Tamil, means small, young. Bokar is a modification of the Arabic name Abū Bakr.

2. Nizam Shah was one of the emperors of the Nizam Shahi dynasty that ruled over territories around Hyderabad in the modern Andhra Pradesh. Nizam Shahs were also known as the Deccan emperors. Ahmad Nagar is the name of a district as well as its headquarters in Maharashtra.

[Note by Nainar] Nizam Shah (Murtaza Nizam Shah) was the Sultan of Ahmad Nagar between 1565 and 1588. During the early years of his reign the affairs of the kingdom were controlled by his mother.

In 1570 Nizam Shah and Ali Adil Shah of Bijapur cooperated with the Zamorin of Calicut to drive out the Portuguese from Goa and Chaul, and divide their possessions. Ali Adil Shah besieged Goa while Murtaza besieged Chaul. But both of them were frustrated in their attempts. The nobles of Nizam Shah betrayed him by not only supplying the Portuguese with intelligence but also with provisions.[Nainar]

3. It was following this request from Adil Shah that the campaign that ended up in the martyrdom of Kuttipocker was undertaken. The Zamorin was then in the midst of the battle of Chaliyam. Therefore, he could not extend timely help to Adil Shah. The forces under Kuttipocker arrived at Chaul and turned back after waiting there for about twenty days. On their return they had a confrontation with the Portuguese forces near Kannur, who were coming towards them in fifteen ships. Kuttipocker was martyred in this confrontation.

Chapter Thirteen

1 The fort the Portuguese viceroy Nuno da Acquina built at Chaliyam in 1531 along with its premises was handed over to Parappanatu Rajah, king of Chaliyam, by the Zamorin in 1571. It took about four months of continuous struggle to evict the Portuguese from there. The leader of the vanguard fighters who led the Zamorin to victory in this battle was Pattumarakkar alias Kunhali III. Following that, the Zamorin gave Kunhali III permission to build a fort at Putupattanam. Kunhali quite vigilantly organized a very good force with people from the coastal belt to fight the Portuguese. He did so because he was quite aware of the Portuguese sense of revenge.

Chapter Fourteen

1. Talaimannar is in the Ramanad district in Karnataka.

2. This might be Galicia, on the northwest tip of Spain. Halatia earlier included territories like La Corona, Lo Gea, Orense, and Pontevedra. Portugal was on the western border of Spain and their mutual relationship is quite understandable. In 1580 Portugal and Spain merged and became one nation. All through the fifteenth century AD, Spain was under the influence of Islam. The Muslims had used Halatia as their operational base for their struggle against the Portuguese. It is quite likely that several Muslims of Halatia came to Malabar at a time when the anti-Portuguese struggle was gathering momentum in Malabar.

3. Sūrah al-Ṭalāq: 65:7 and Sūrah al-Sharḥ: 94:5-6.

4. This Akbar Badshah was the famous Mughal emperor Abul-Fatah Jalaluddin Muhammad (1542-1608 AD). He was son of the Mughal emperor Humayun.

5. Adilabad is in the modern Andhra Pradesh.

6. Dabul or Dabol is an ancient city south of modern Mumbai. It is situated on the northern bank of the Wasishta River in Ratnagiri district, south of the Chaul port and north of Sintapur.

7. This extract is drawn from Sūrah al-Nisā': 75 in the Qur'an. The first part of this verse is explained in Endnote no. 17 of Section 1.

8. This is the treaty the Zamorin had with the Portuguese viceroy Francisco Mascaranus. Mascaranus was appointed the viceroy by the Spanish emperor Philip following the merger of Portugal and Spain in 1580 AD.

9. This treaty would have been of some temporary relief to the Muslims. But the selfish and crooked Portuguese had certain hidden goals behind it. But Kunhali III, who could see through this on time, did not accept this and continued the struggle against the Portuguese along with his followers. And the Portuguese on their side too continued their atrocities on the Muslims even while they were in a treaty with the Portuguese. In 1580 AD a fierce battle took place between Kunhali III and the Portuguese. Following this, Khawajah Musa, nephew of Kunhali III, seized all the ships the Portuguese had set sail at sea. Unable to win over Kunhali III in the struggle, the Portuguese again made a treaty with the Zamorin in 1591 AD. Kunhali III was enraged and in another battle with the Portuguese they again violated the terms of the treaty. But being quite old, he could not personally involve in the confrontations for long. He was forced to hand over the responsibilities to his nephew Muhammad Ali. In 1595 AD Kunhali III died of old age and his nephew Muhammad Ali took charge as Kunhali IV, the new military chief of the Zamorin. His first major concern was rebuilding the Putuppanam fort in a cleverer and more

strategically effective way. At this juncture, the scheming Portuguese succeeded in propitiating the feeble-minded Zamorin. They frightened him saying that if he did not capture Kunhali's fort in Putuppanam, Kunhali will depose him from power and will rule over his country before long. Thus the Zamorin and the Portuguese joined hands to confront Kunhali IV. Initially they had a lot of setbacks. In 1599, the Portuguese forces that had come from Goa with massive military preparations and the Zamorin's forces together attacked Kunhali IV and his followers from land as well as sea. Kunhali IV virtually had no way out. He surrendered voluntarily to the Zamorin on 16 March 1600 on condition that they will not jeopardise their lives and that they will be let free to go. It is said that when the Portuguese chief Furtado held his hand, Kunhali knocked him down. Eventually, the Portuguese, quite treacherously and against the terms of the treaty, took Kunhali, his nephew, and his followers to Goa and beheaded them there. They hacked Kunhali's corpse into four and exhibited it on the beach and sent his head, salted and dried in the sun, to Kannur.

The elimination of the four Kunhalis facilitated things for the Portuguese. However, other European forces arrived in Malabar before long and the Portuguese had to meet them. What finally destroyed the decades-long Portuguese occupation of Malabar was the arrival of the Dutch in 1663. Not more than four years after the murder of Kunhali, the Zamorin had a treaty with the Dutch to evict the Portuguese not only from his territory but from India altogether.

Index of Persons and Places